338.7764   Amos, Wally
The cookie never crumbles

WITHDRAWN

The Cookie Never Crumbles

Wally Amos

and

Eden-Lee Murray

The Cookie Never Crumbles

St. Martin's Press ❧ New York

www.stmartins.com

ISBN 0-312-28032-7

First Edition: October 2001

10   9   8   7   6   5   4   3   2   1

To Ruth Wakefield,
the creator of the
Tollhouse Chocolate Chip Cookie,
and Aunt Della—
my two chocolate chip cookie angels

Contents

4: First Courses: Famous Amos Start-up

5: Entrées: Famous Amos Full-Tilt

10: Time-Honored Cookie Recipes

Acknowledgments

I am more inclined to give thanks than to acknowledge. To acknowledge is to recognize. To give thanks is to express gratitude, and I am most grateful for those who helped publish this book. Let me name them and tell you why I'm grateful.

I first give thanks to God, who gives me each breath, which enables me to do everything I do.

Thanks to Neale Donald Walsch for convincing me to write the book and then for giving me a great title, *The Cookie Never Crumbles.*

Thanks to Jerry Jamposky and Diane Cirincione for inviting me to their house for dinner with Neale and his wife, Nancy. It was here that the seed for the book was planted.

Thanks to Roger Jellinek for finding me a publisher and for being so supportive during the process. Thanks also for introducing me to my coauthor, Eden-Lee Murray.

Eden-Lee, you were fantastic to work with. Thanks for giving life to my stories. You are a blessing.

When you look in the dictionary for the definition of the word *editor*, you should see a picture of Jennifer Enderlin. Jen, thanks for your great enthusiasm and wonderful editorial skills.

A huge thanks to my wife, Christine, for her patience and support.

Thanks to everyone at St. Martin's Press who had anything to do with the publication of this book. I greatly appreciate your efforts.

Thanks to all the booksellers. Without you, books would not be published.

Finally, to you, the customer. You are the reason we write books. Thank you for buying *The Cookie Never Crumbles.*

Foreword

I want to tell you about one of the most extraordinary men I have ever met. His name is Wally Amos. What makes Wally extraordinary is not anything that he has done, but what he *is*. And I can say what he is in one word:

Happy.

Now maybe you expected a "bigger" word, or a "more important" word. Maybe you expected me to say that Wally Amos is *profound* or *enlightened* or *wise* or *compassionate* or *understanding* or *kind* or *generous* or *remarkable*, or something *larger* than simply "happy." Yet, when I look at life closely I realize that there is *nothing* larger than "happy."

Everything else we do is an attempt to be *that*.

Wally Amos is a happy man. He is probably the most consistently happy person that I have ever known. Because he has found the Secret of Happiness, I believe him also to be profound, enlightened, wise, compassionate, understanding, kind, generous, and remarkable. And a great deal more.

Wally is happy not only when things look good, but also when things look like what you and I would call "bad." He is happy not only when the sun in shining, but when the wind is blowing as well. He reminds me of a wonderful statement by famed psychiatrist Dr. Elisabeth Kubler-Ross: "Should you shield the canyon from the windstorms, you would never see the beauty of their carvings."

Wally Amos is a beautiful man, not because he's led a beautiful life, but because he has seen beauty in the life he's led. And now, here comes this beautiful man, with his beautiful soul and his beautiful mind, into your life and mine, through this book, to share with us his beautiful message. Here's Wally—and I can see him grinning now, with his impish, dare-you-not-to-like-this grin—telling us not only how to *find* happiness, but how to *create* it. And not only in our own lives, but in the lives of others.

This is, of course, the greatest secret of life. For he who creates happiness everywhere finds it everywhere he goes.

That's what Wally Amos does. I have never seen a room that Wally Amos has entered which did not light up. I have never seen a person he has encountered who did not become better for the experience. And I have never, *ever* known a person who was discouraged who could *remain* discouraged in Wally Amos's presence for more than five minutes.

Now, I want you to read this book. I have read it, and I am going to read it over and over and over again because it lifts my soul and warms my heart and opens my mind and lightens my burden. And I want that for you, too.

Read this book, and come to know the simple truths that will bring you the simple experience of the greatest thing that life has to offer: happiness.

Another title which could have been given this book is *A Recipe for Happiness,* by one of the greatest chefs of all time. So sit down now and look at these recipes. Study them, and don't be fooled by their simplicity. This is powerful stuff here. From these recipes you can make of your life a beautiful banquet.

—Neale Donald Walsch, author of *Conversations with God*

Introduction

Aloha!

So, you think you're holding a cookbook. Well, in the larger sense of the word, you are; but the truth is, the book you've got in your hands goes far beyond offering recipes for tasty edibles! These are recipes for the delicious successes you can whip up in your own life, if you have the right ingredients!

The one thing I've done more than anything else in my life is bake cookies. When Neale Donald Walsch suggested the title of this book, *The Cookie Never Crumbles*, it occurred to me that there's a whole lot we can all learn from cookies.

Just to give you an example: How many times in our lives have we heard the phrase, "Well, that's the way the cookie crumbles," in connection with a disappointment or failure? It's supposed to make us feel better, right? Whatever it was we were hoping for just wasn't meant to be; it was destined to crumble and fall apart, just like a cookie.

Well that logic just doesn't hold water. It totally slanders the nature of a cookie! When a cookie breaks apart, you don't lose the cookie, you get lots of little cookies. They smell just as good and taste just as good as their larger brothers and sisters. The fact that a cookie can break into tinier and tinier pieces and still retain all of its wonderful characteristics is a tremendous attribute. The cookie is, in fact, indestructible!

Now it is my pleasure to pass these life-enhancing recipes on to you with the conviction that we all have it in us to be brilliant cooks in our own life-kitchens. It seems so obvious, but for some reason, people need to be reminded of their tremendous potential for excellence, creativity, and productivity. Consider me your friendly reminder!

As you know, one of the best things about sharing recipes is that they can always be adapted and adjusted to fit your own needs and tastes; and remember, whatever happens with cookies, it's always for the best.

Enjoy!

1

Welcome to My Kitchen

Essential Ingredients for Your Personal Pantry

All good cooks will tell you the key to their success is the quality of their ingredients. With a comprehensive selection of high-grade herbs, spices, seasonings, and condiments at their fingertips, there is little they cannot accomplish. So it is with us in terms of the ingredients we have at our command to create useful, successful, "gourmet" lives.

Challenges over the years have taught me, one by one, the essential ingredients I've needed to bring into my kitchen to stock what I call my Personal Pantry. Let us consider these indispensables as our "spices for life." I'll group and list them here, and then show you how I've used them in the recipes that follow:

Basics

These ingredients are key in just about any recipe you undertake—like salt. Even when they're not specifically mentioned in the recipes/situations that follow, you can bet a good cook will be sure to include them in varying proportions, as needed:

Honesty, Integrity, Positive Loving Attitude, Faith, Fun, Responsibility, Commitment, Reality, Imagination, Energy,

Serendipity (common name: Luck), Intuition, Humility, Giving, (a.k.a. unconditional sharing of self).

Survival Spices

As their name implies, these spices are the ones that will see you through just about any kind of challenge:

Unconditional Love, Spirituality, Self-Respect, Trust, Determination, Clarity, Balance, Courage, Self-Awareness, Confidence, Tenacity (common name: Stick-to-it-iveness), Indefatigability, Resourcefulness, Perspective, Good Judgment, Practicality, Relationships.

Entrepreneurial Extracts

These are what you should keep in stock to concoct successful business enterprises:

Superlative Mentors, Teamwork, Individuality, Enthusiasm, Vitality, Personality, Decisiveness, Leadership, Passion, Vision, Originality, Forthrightness, Ability to Focus on Answers/Solutions, Networking Skills, Willingness to Work Hard (common name: Elbow Grease), Productivity, Competence, Problem-Solving Skills, Attention to Detail, Self-Sufficiency, Thrift.

Relationship Relishes

These are the ingredients that keep friends and loved ones around your table:

> Generosity, Ability to Receive, Respect, Tolerance, Friendship, Spontaneity, Playfulness, Appreciation, Thoughtfulness, Gentleness, Amiability, Fair-Mindedness, Credibility, Forbearance, Empathy, Loyalty, Sensitivity, Active Listening.

Cook's Note: It may seem that some of the ingredients in my Personal Pantry are contradictory, but you know, when you get ready to create a dish, you rarely, if ever, use everything at your disposal! It all depends on what you want to cook. Meat dishes call for herbs and spices that are totally inappropriate for cakes and cookies. On the other hand, I don't think I know many recipes that can do without at least a pinch of salt.

In life, as in the kitchen, balance and adjustment are everything, and almost everyone I know tweaks even their tried-and-true recipes, adjusting them a smidge every time they prepare them. Circumstances always dictate what you choose to use, but the point is to make sure you have what you need in stock!

The Golden Rule of Recipes

As we start off on this adventure together, I'd like to offer this thought as a fundamental touchstone for the art of recipe creating.

Here's the bottom line for any recipe: Specific combinations of Ingredients A, B, C, and so on are going to result in Product X. If you, the cook, are not satisfied with Product X, it is up to you to alter the combination and proportions of the ingredients that you selected. If your final product pleases you, then you'd better pay attention to what you used to create it.

Now, since what I'm talking about are Recipes for Life, how can we apply this Golden Rule to who we are and what we do? It's simple! If all the events of your life—your ingredients—have combined to produce the person you are today, and if you are happy with those results, then it stands to reason that you've got a successful recipe going: A, B, and C produced an X you like. This approach can make us all much more accepting of what happens in our lives. Even when some stuff doesn't feel too good at the time it goes into the mix, it can still ultimately be part of something very tasty. In many cases, what tastes bitter by itself adds depth and richness to a dish.

By the same token, if you're disappointed in Product X, then you'd better rethink the ABCs of your ingredients. It's always a question of balancing the recipe 'til you get what you want. Just remember: You're the cook!

"Kiss the Cook!"

We've all seen this slogan emblazoned/embroidered/printed on various kitchen accoutrements, whether aprons, oven mitts or dish towels. But let's look at this cliché with fresh eyes. There's something important to pay attention to here.

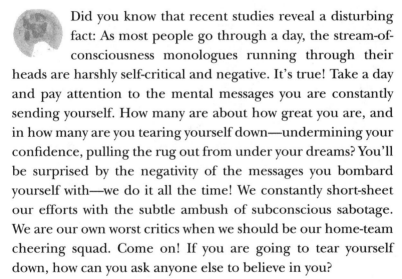 Did you know that recent studies reveal a disturbing fact: As most people go through a day, the stream-of-consciousness monologues running through their heads are harshly self-critical and negative. It's true! Take a day and pay attention to the mental messages you are constantly sending yourself. How many are about how great you are, and in how many are you tearing yourself down—undermining your confidence, pulling the rug out from under your dreams? You'll be surprised by the negativity of the messages you bombard yourself with—we do it all the time! We constantly short-sheet our efforts with the subtle ambush of subconscious sabotage. We are our own worst critics when we should be our home-team cheering squad. Come on! If you are going to tear yourself down, how can you ask anyone else to believe in you?

So I'm saying, "Kiss the cook"—and that means you! Change those negative tapes playing in your head to positive, encouraging ones, so you are constantly reminding yourself that in the kitchen of your life, you are the manifestation of God's light.

 Cook's Note: If you believe, there's nothing you cannot achieve!

Light That Fire!

It's impossible to pick out the single most important ingredient for a Personal Pantry, but there's one you must have on hand if you want to accomplish anything, and that is Commitment.

So many times people say, "I *hope* such-and-such will happen . . ." or "I'll *try* to do it." *No!!!* "Hoping" and "trying" do not bring recipes to fruition—Commitment does. After you've made your plans, mixed your batter, and dropped your dough onto the cookie sheet, nothing's going to happen unless you turn on the oven. Commitment is the match that lights the fire.

Goethe, the brilliant poet/philosopher, put this truth beautifully. Tuck his words in your Personal Pantry as a reminder:

Until one is committed, there is hesitancy, the chance to draw back, always ineffectiveness. Concerning all acts of initiative (and creation), there is one elementary truth, the ignorance of which kills countless ideas and splendid plans: that the moment one definitely commits oneself, then providence moves, too.

All sorts of things occur to help one that never would otherwise have happened. A whole stream of events issues from the decision, raising in one's favor all manner of unforeseen incidents and meetings and material assistance, which no man could have dreamed would have come his way.

Are you in earnest? Seek this very minute whatever you

can do, or dream you can, begin it. Boldness has genius, power, and magic in it. Only engage and the mind grows heated, begin and then the task will be completed.

> ***Cook's Note:*** You can't bake anything unless you turn your oven on. *"I will do this!"* is an affirmation that makes the whole universe rejoice, and with that commitment, you will find the universe conspiring to help you achieve your goal.

About Cookie Notes

Let's take a moment to sing the praises of an often underused ingredient: Appreciation. Most of us are pretty handy at giving critical feedback in response to a performance we find lacking in some respect. But how many of us take the time to acknowledge something that works?

There's a great saying, "Water the rose, and let the weeds die." The truth about human behavior is that people live either up to or down to expectations. When you let people know you appreciate something they've done, they naturally feel good about themselves as a result. That boost to self-esteem translates directly to a higher level of performance.

A Cookie Note doesn't have to be elaborate or earthshaking. It can be something as simple as "Gee, I really liked the energy you brought to that meeting—you created a positive tone right from the start."

Now, the really neat thing about giving a Cookie Note is that it lifts spirits on both sides of the exchange! By choosing to make others feel good about themselves, you find you feel terrific, too—use it! It works if you work it!

Cook's Note: Just as giving people cookies provides physical nourishment, offering them a Cookie Note generates morale-boosting emotional energy. Definitely a win-win combination.

2

Family Recipes

The Tao of the Cookie

The following is one of my favorite fables, and offers a terrific frame of reference for the Family Recipes that follow.

Once upon a time, in ancient China, there lived a Taoist farmer who followed the Great Way to God. He was considered a wealthy man because he had a horse to help with plowing. One early spring morning, his horse ran off. When the villagers heard, they hastened to his home to express their sympathy. "What a terrible thing!" they lamented.

But all the Taoist farmer said was, "Maybe."

The next morning, his horse returned, leading an entire herd of wild mustangs. The townspeople rushed over, exclaiming at his good fortune. "Now you are the richest man in the province!" they exulted.

But all the farmer said was, "Maybe."

The following morning, the farmer's only son awoke at dawn to begin breaking one of the wild horses. It promptly threw him, and his leg was broken. The townspeople rushed over in alarm. "What a terrible thing!" they wept. "Without the help of your only son, how can you plant your fields?"

But all the farmer said was, "Maybe."

The next afternoon, the emperor's soldiers rode into town, kicking up an enormous cloud of dust. They had come to conscript all the young men to fight a war, but the farmer's son could not go because of his broken leg. The townspeople once again gathered around to marvel at the farmer's good luck.

But, just as before, he only shook his head at their foolish excitement, and all he said was, "Maybe."

Although the fable continues through a long series of alternating downturns and upturns, the farmer's reaction does not vary. He never lets himself be swayed emotionally in either direction, but instead stays balanced, poised to accept and weave whatever may come his way into his life.

The old farmer's attitude may strike us as passive, but there is great power in his understatement. In his wisdom, he understood that each step in the "recipe" that was unfolding around him was neither good nor bad in and of itself, but merely part of the ongoing oneness of life flowing along inexorably.

In her book *The Ways of the Mystic,* Dr. Joan Borysenko puts it this way: ". . . all things conspire creatively for life to grow and evolve. Incidents that appear either good or bad can never be judged in isolation. Life is a paradox in which all things are relative and interrelated."

As you'll see in the following recipes, sometimes when a dish seems to be off to an inauspicious start, there are nevertheless forces at work that ultimately result in a successful outcome.

Tao Recipe for Life

Start with a large measure of *Faith*: Know that you are here for a purpose, whether or not you understand specifically what it is.

Add a hearty cup of *Acceptance*: Whatever happens to you happens for a reason, and there is a lesson to be learned.

Stir in a tablespoon of *Patience*: Trust in the abundance of the Universe and the wisdom of God.

The final ingredient is a generous sprinkling of *Balance*: Stay equally centered in the face of either extraordinarily good or bad fortune.

The beauty of this recipe is that it lasts and lasts and lasts!

Loving Cup

More often than not, the relationship we have with one or the other of our parents is the prototype for every subsequent relationship we experience. This was certainly true for me, and accepting that fundamental relationship with unconditional love proved to be the recipe for success in every other relationship in my life!

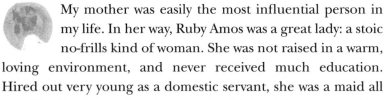My mother was easily the most influential person in my life. In her way, Ruby Amos was a great lady: a stoic no-frills kind of woman. She was not raised in a warm, loving environment, and never received much education. Hired out very young as a domestic servant, she was a maid all her life. She had a ferocious work ethic and from my earliest days she impressed upon me the value of discipline, hard work, and doing my very best no matter what the job was.

My mother had extremely high ideals, and boy was she a tough taskmaster! You could say she was one tough cookie. Whenever I failed to measure up to her expectations, she whipped me, all the while maintaining that the beatings hurt her more than they did me. As a child, I couldn't understand that logic; but much later, as an adult, I was at least able to see her point of view. She took her maternal responsibility very seriously, and the only way she knew how to demonstrate her love for me was through her zealous discipline. While she certainly could never have been accused of indifference, the words "I love you" were never uttered in our house.

Looking back at my childhood, it's so easy to see how we were at cross-purposes. She and I simply had unrealistic expectations of each other: She wanted to raise a responsible, hard-working, clean-living successful son—what mother doesn't? But given her impossible ideals, nothing I could do was ever good enough. My only reward for my efforts was negativity and criticism. By the same token, however, she was not the loving Ideal Mother I fantasized about, and her having to clean other people's houses for a living was always a disappointment to me. Instead of appreciating all her hard work on my behalf, I longed for her to be something other than what she was, and with the heartless egocentricity of a child, I'm sure I let her know it. My attitude must have hurt her deeply.

As I got older, my solution to our impasse was to spend as little time as possible in her presence; but even at a distance, the pattern of expectation, disappointment, and criticism continued in our relationship.

Here's where it gets interesting. Not only was I incapable of resolving my relationship with Ruby, but by now I was finding the same kind of pattern in other relationships: expectation, disappointment, frustration, withdrawal. My first two marriages failed because I didn't understand the first thing about unconditional love. I was willing to give love, but it had to be on my terms. With Ruby as my role model, I'd never learned how to be gentle or supportive. I found myself on the other side of the equation, repeating the pattern with my children—and my strictness with them produced the very same reaction Ruby's had with me: resistance and withdrawal!

In my forty-first year, however, I had a soul blowing epiphany. For whatever reason, I was able to see clearly for the first time that my job as Ruby's son was just to love her. My intention became not to change her, not to wish her to be different, but to love and accept the Ruby that was, simply because she was my mother. You cannot believe how liberating that realization was! From that moment on, I stopped criticizing and correcting her, and resolved to deal with her from a positive, loving perspective. I tuned out anything negative when we spoke, and made it a point to close all of our phone conversations with "I love you, Mama."

And do you know what? When I changed my attitude and my behavior with her, she began to change toward me! She got to where she'd respond to my "I love you's" with her own pure, heartfelt "I love you, too, Baby." See, the thing is, she had loved me all along, but I had defended myself from her way of expressing it, which in turn made her angry and defensive. When I finally dropped my guard and allowed her love to get to me, there was no more resistance for her to overcome, and our love could flow back and forth freely between us. I thank God that we were able to become friends at last. She died in 1994, but I still have a relationship with her. People die, relationships don't, and as long as I live, she will live on through me.

It took the power of unconditional love to resolve that fundamental relationship. Then the "trickle-down" phenomenon kicked in. Little by little, the lesson I had learned with Ruby began to impact the other relationships in my life. Old patterns began to shift, and I noticed improvements in the way others related to me. As a result, I had another great epiphany: We are in charge of how people respond to us, not the other way around!

This realization has transformed every relationship in my life, from my marriage, to my children, to my friends and business associates. It is such a relief to accept the people in your life, to love them for who they are. When you operate from a perspective of abundant, unconditional love, you cannot lose! Love is nothing until you give it away, and the more you give, the more you get. Giving is Receiving!

Recipe for Successful Relationships

Gently mix together Equal Quantities of *Unconditional Love, Acceptance, Non-Judgment, Positive Loving Attitude, Faith, Appreciation, Gentleness, Empathy,* and *Friendship*

Just before serving, garnish with *Spirituality* to remind all who partake that we are spiritual beings having human experiences, not the other way around.

This dish should be shared with loving concern and sensitivity.

 Cook's Note: Whatever the question, Love is the answer!

Loving Cup Postscript

Here's a little story that exemplifies the power of Unconditional Love and Acceptance.

I was with a wonderful friend of mine, Albert Roker, when he and his lovely wife Bessie celebrated their fiftieth wedding anniversary. They amazed me: From the tender, romantic way they related to each other they could have been newlyweds!

I said to him, "Albert, fifty years is a long time! How on earth have you managed to stay so loving after being married for half a century?!"

I'll never forget his answer. He looked at me and replied simply, "Wally, I accept her."

That says it all!

Lovin' Spoonfuls

"DIVORCE." Now, there's a word that strikes terror into any kid's heart. It's an experience that means separation and loss, major life changes, and emotional upheaval. It can scar for life. In my case, however, it opened up a whole realm of possibilities, and paved the way for this recipe!

In 1948, the gap that had been widening between my parents for some time passed the point of no return, and they decided to end their marriage. Our home had been in Tallahassee, Florida, and my father stayed there while my mother moved the both of us to Orlando. One month later, she sent me to New York City to live with my Aunt Della, her husband, Fred, and their son, Joe.

In one short month, I'd lost my parents, my home, my friends, my community—in short, everything that had defined me up to that point. I was twelve at the time. Now, child psychologists agree that's about the worst time in a young boy's life for divorce to occur. I certainly didn't need an expert to tell me I felt bad.

Although I certainly didn't feel it at the time, I was really very lucky. Aunt Della, Fred, and Joe welcomed me into their tiny little one bedroom apartment at 567 West 161st Street in West Harlem. Joe shared his room—the living room—with me. I thank God for Aunt Della! She knew I was hurting. She loved me, she accepted me, and she baked me cookies. Chocolate Chip Cookies. No one had ever baked me chocolate chip cookies before. They were just magic. Now, I know that part of that magic was sitting there in that teensy little kitchen, which was hardly bigger than a box, watching Aunt Della mix up a batch; helping her when the spoon and bowl needed licking, and then biting into those warm, chewy morsels as soon as they were cool enough to handle. Comfort food, for sure. All Aunt Della needed was to see me with a sad face, and *boom!* Into the kitchen for cookies.

It was an easy step for me to connect the pleasure of eating those cookies with the comfort and security of her love. Long after I'd come through the worst pain of my parents' divorce, and had more or less adjusted to my new life, my emotional connection to chocolate chip cookies stayed with me.

My parent's divorce could have crippled me emotionally, but instead, thanks to Aunt Della's unconditional love—and my ability to receive it—that time in my life actually formed the profound connection for what was ultimately going to lead to my first huge success: The Cookie!

Recipe for The Cookie That Never Crumbles

Take basic mix for twelve-year-old boy.

Add 2–3 cups of bitter chocolate chips of *Experience*.

Carefully sweeten with large measures of *Unconditional Love*, tasting frequently to adjust the balance.

Let the mixture mature in warm, nurturing environment to ensure *Receptivity* of the mix.

When mix is ready, drop loving spoonfuls onto cookie sheet, and bake til done. Don't be afraid of the heat. It's what transforms the raw dough into the finished product— a necessary part of the process.

Result: A healthy treat to share with the world.

3

Hors D'oeuvres

On Being a Sous-Chef, 4:

As they say, you have to learn to crawl before you can walk, and walk before you can run. But how do you get the idea to stand up in the first place? By watching someone who's already learned how! It's no different with each new challenge in life—your goal must be to find someone who excels at what you want to do, and put yourself in a position to learn from their experience!

In November 1957, following my honorable discharge from the U.S. Air Force, I was hired by Saks Fifth Avenue as a temporary stock clerk in the supply room. The job was to be only for the duration of the holiday season. Nevertheless, when I accepted it, I was determined to be the very best temporary supply-department stock clerk Saks had ever employed!

My job included unloading packing cartons from trucks, receiving and storing office supplies, policing areas where cartons were kept to make sure they were stacked neatly, and delivering supplies to departments throughout the store. I worked hard with the same enthusiasm and energy I've brought to any project I've ever undertaken. Without being asked, I even reorganized the supply department to improve the system and make it more efficient. I always looked to go at least one step further than what was asked of me. The manager, a splendid human being named Ernie Riccio, was so pleased with my work that he arranged for my job to continue part-time after the holidays.

Ernie was my first real mentor. He took me under his wing, becoming a father figure, and a wonderful friend as well. Not only did he see to it that I got the stockroom job on a permanent basis, he took it upon himself to educate me. I noticed that he read all the major business publications, and when I asked him why, he said, "Because you have to be informed about what's going on around you! You're working in a big store, right? Well, what's happening in the world of business directly affects your paycheck!"

Thanks to him I discovered the world of finance, reading the *Wall Street Journal, U.S. News & World Report*, and other important business journals. Then we would discuss the articles I'd read. Although neither of us knew it at the time, he primed my pump by exposing me to information that would eventually benefit my own business endeavors.

Watching Ernie manage his "kitchen" at Saks taught me a lot about the ingredients I wanted in my own Personal Pantry. I stayed with Saks for four years and worked my way up to Ernie Riccio's job, with his blessing!

Cook's Note: The ingredients I brought into this situation were a *Positive Mental Attitude, Energy, Enthusiasm*, an appetite for *Problem Solving*, and an *Eagerness to Learn*. Ernie was able to take those ingredients and, using his skills as a master chef, turn me into a far better employee.

This was one instance where the "chef" I studied under taught me by positive example. That's not always the case, but negative examples can be useful, too—it's much less painful to learn from someone else's mistakes!

Ultimatum Dip

My first job in the "real world" was in the supply department of Saks Fifth Avenue, where I started off as the most temporary of temporary employees, stayed four years, and worked my way up to the position of manager. It would have been easy to kick back and settle for that, but something told me there had to be more to my life than that—greater Kitchens were calling and, hard as it was at the time, I had to listen!

By the time I left Saks Fifth Avenue, I was manager of the supply department, with my very own gold Saks Executive Identification Card, and a weekly salary of $85. During my four years there, I had become a family man, and now had a wife, a two-year-old son, and another baby on the way. My weekly paycheck of $85 just wasn't enough. Plus by then I needed some tangible demonstration from Saks of their appreciation. It was a question of morale almost as much as money.

I approached Saks for a $10 a week raise. It didn't seem like too much to ask, given the quality of job performance they were getting from me. I was even prepared to accept half that amount, but it was not to be. Saks said no. My only option, as I saw it then, was to give my two weeks' notice as an ultimatum if they did not agree to even the smaller raise. I was hoping that the threat of losing my valuable services would motivate the powers that be at Saks to reconsider their decision. They remained unmoved. The answer was still no.

Now, the thing I learned about ultimatums is that if you make one, and the other party doesn't acquiesce, then there you are. You either have to put up or shut up, as the saying goes. I'd taken my stand, drawn my line in the sand, and lost. Now I had to make a tough decision. I could go through with my ultimatum, leave the job, and face unemployment with a pregnant wife and toddler to feed, clothe and shelter. Or I could swallow my pride and stay. I felt that if I stayed, I might just as well chain myself to a post in that supply room. I knew which option I had to choose to be able to live with myself.

On August 11, 1961, I quit the job. And do you know what? Every August 11 I feel like sending Saks a thank-you card! Had they given in to my ultimatum, I'd probably have been content to serve out my career in that stockroom—who knows what would have become of me? You can never know what would have happened "if . . ." But I can just about guarantee that my getting that raise would have derailed the sequence of events that eventually produced Famous Amos!

Cook's Note: There is no sweetener that can make an ultimatum easy to swallow, but here are the ingredients you want to make sure you have on hand before you offer one:

Judgment: Be sure the situation calls for an ultimatum. This is not a tactic to use lightly.

Decisiveness: Make an honest evaluation of your situation, and be clear about what you want to accomplish.

Fairness: Create and offer a solution that is win-win all around.

Confidence and *Courage*: Stand firm and believe in yourself, even if your ultimatum is rejected. DO NOT BACK DOWN!

Faith: Trust that if you do not achieve your goal with the ultimatum, there is always something better waiting for you. As Richard Cohn of Beyond Words Publishing puts it: "We are standing in possibilities!"

Navigating a Buffet Line:

OR, BEFORE YOU PUT IT ON YOUR PLATE, BE SURE YOU WANT TO EAT IT!

Some would say there are two ways of looking at being out of work: The Pessimist says, "Damn! I just lost my job! I'm unemployed! Aughhhhhh!" The Optimist says, "Whoooeee—look at this great vacation between jobs!"

If, however, you share my view of the universe as one of infinite abundance, you go way beyond the Optimist and see all kinds of opportunities ready to fill the void that appears when you leave a job! One caution, however, is not to jump at the first opportunity that presents itself, but to wait instead, and trust that the right opportunity for you *will present itself. I learned this the hard way!*

I walked away from my first steady job in the Saks Fifth Avenue supply room, when management denied me a well-deserved raise in pay. My choice was to stay in what would most likely have turned out to be a dead-end position, or quit and see what else might be available to a young man of my energy and ambition. During this time posters for the *New York Times* were plastered all over the subways: they all had somebody who looked really happy holding up the help-wanted section, saying, "I got my job through the *New York Times.*" I figured, that's it! I'll get my job through the *New York Times*!

I took a week off to be with my family, and then I turned to the *Times* and hit the pavement. I visited a lot of offices and had a lot of job possibilities—I was very well qualified for clerical/secretarial positions, thanks to my work at Collegiate, a fine New York City business school that offered topflight secretarial training—but there just wasn't anything that was particularly attractive to me.

At one point I considered working for the Sanitation Department, but I didn't think about it for very long. It was summertime, and the idea of working around the smell of hot garbage just didn't appeal to me. It wasn't much better in winter, either: In winter, those guys have to shovel snow to get to the garbage! I said to myself, no, I don't want to do that, so the Sanitation Department was out.

Then I thought maybe I'd drive a cab. My uncle Fred had driven a cab. I figured cabdrivers make good money—they work long hours, but how bad could that be? I actually went down to the Hack Bureau, the New York City department in charge of regulating and licensing taxi companies, and started filling out the application. Then it hit me: "I just don't want to drive a cab!" So I left.

My options were diminishing, as was my bank balance. For a brief period, I even sold vacuum cleaners door-to-door. I'd been supplementing my income by selling mutual funds, so I decided to go ahead and see if I could sell life insurance as well.

The Aetna Insurance Company sponsored me to take their exam, which was in St. Nicholas Arena on Columbus Avenue in Manhattan. This was a *huge* place—they used to have boxing matches in there—and on this occasion it was almost filled with people taking this qualifying exam. Now, the line from insurance companies recruiting salespeople was that on the whole, most people out there are underinsured. Looking around the room I said to myself: "*All* these people are in here, taking this exam to be able to go out and sell insurance—how many are already out there selling insurance?!" It was not a thrilling thought, but with a family to feed, I went ahead and took the exam, even though my heart was definitely not in selling life insurance for a living. While waiting to hear my results Collegiate Secretarial School called me about an opening they wanted me to interview for at the William Morris talent agency. Now, that sounded interesting!

My point here is that there were numerous opportunities to settle for a solution that would have solved my problem, which was unemployment. But I just couldn't see committing myself to something I felt halfhearted about doing, right from the outset. That would have been unfair to both my employer and myself. And, had I not held out for something that really piqued my interest, I'd have never been available for the fourteen-year career in show business that the interview at William Morris was about to launch!

As it turned out, what I learned at the agency, and even later from my experience as an independent personal-talent manager positioned me beautifully for kicking off Famous Amos with a bang!

Buffetgoer's Guide

It's always wise to scout what's available on the table, but don't fill up your plate with stuff you only sort-of want, just to put something on it. Hold out for a dish that's both nutritious and delicious for your life, then go for it!

Starting from Scratch

Sometimes it's tempting to balk at an opportunity because it looks like you have to take two steps back instead of moving forward as you think you should. But if you accept the perspective of a Greater Force in the Universe at work, you can see that that's not always a bad thing. You can never know when key elements are being moved into position to push you forward—sometimes you just have to trust.

Between the years of 1957 and 1961, I'd been getting started on a lot of fronts: I was working my way up in my first job in the supply department of Saks Fifth Avenue; I'd gotten married and started a family. I hadn't paid a lot of attention to what was going on in the world around me, and hadn't focused on the fact that the civil-rights movement had been steadily gaining strength across the country. By 1961, the movement's leaders were aggressively attempting to raise the consciousness of major companies.

Frustrated at what I perceived as indifference and a lack of appreciation from my employers at Saks, I gave my notice of resignation, and started job hunting in a whole new world— an environment in which corporations were being harshly criticized for racist hiring policies. Perhaps the unlikeliest (but most intriguing!) interview I had was at the William Morris Agency, one of the largest theatrical agencies in the entertainment industry, and one that had just been singled out as a prime perpetrator of racial discrimination. While it had the largest roster of black entertainers—Sammy Davis, Jr.

headed the list—there was not one black agent. Never had been.

Enter Wally Amos: singularly underqualified for the agent's job I was interviewing for. *But* I was black—they needed me! It was a question of being the right color, at the right place, at the right time. I saw a whole new realm of possibilities opening up for me. This was the first career opportunity I'd seen that I'd really been excited about.

As it came to pass, I didn't get hired as an agent right off the bat—how could I be? I had no experience in show business whatsoever! But I did get hired, and entered the entertainment industry through the very backest of back doors: I came in as a messenger in the William Morris mailroom, which was a point of entry for new hires of any color. I'd gone from being the manager of the supply department at Saks, earning $85 a week, to mailroom gofer taking a $35 a week pay cut. But, sometimes you have to set your ego aside to accomplish your long-term objectives.

I set my goal, and during the course of the following year, worked my way up from the mailroom, to substitute secretary for senior agents Irwin Winkler and Bernie Brillstein, and then to a permanent secretarial position with Howard Hausman— one of the top executives in the agency who had had the final say in my being hired in the first place.

I delivered the highest-quality job performance I could give. In each position, I took full advantage of the opportunity to learn as much as I possibly could about the inner workings of the agency as well as how the entertainment world operated. As a result, I learned a tremendous amount about the show-business industry in a relatively short period of time. It was with Howard Hausman's blessing that not long after that, I realized my dream of becoming the first black agent ever in the most respected talent agency in the entertainment industry—in less than one year!

Cook's Note: When you're starting from scratch in a new kitchen, be sure to familiarize yourself with the territory. Make a point of getting to know the staff from the ground up.

Spices you want to make sure to have on hand:

Focus—keep your eye on the prize.

Energy—give unstintingly of yourself. Extra effort will be noticed and rewarded.

Preparation and *Confidence*—if you do your homework, you will be more likely to convince the senior chefs to give you a chance at more ambitious dishes.

Courage and *Faith*—dare to put yourself in challenging situations, and trust that you'll have what it takes.

On Being a Sous-Chef, 14:

HOWARD HAUSMAN'S KITCHEN

I have certainly been blessed by special people who have come along at critical junctures in my life. A man named Ernie Riccio was a tremendous mentor to me during my first job at Saks Fifth Avenue, and Howard Hausman at the William Morris Agency was most definitely another. What a wonderful human being!

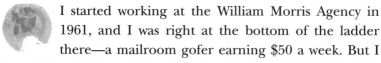 I started working at the William Morris Agency in 1961, and I was right at the bottom of the ladder there—a mailroom gofer earning $50 a week. But I knew I wasn't going to be there for long. I rapidly worked my way out of the mailroom, thanks to my well-honed secretarial skills, and moved quickly from temporary secretarial positions to specifically designated ones. I had faith that I would eventually achieve my goal of becoming a full-fledged agent; but had it not been for a man named Howard Hausman's help and encouragement, I'm sure it would have been a much longer, more arduous climb.

Howard was one of the top executives in the agency—the one who'd had final say in my being hired in the first place. One of my "permanent" secretarial positions was as Howard's assistant, and what an experience that was! He was a remarkable role model in every sense. My biggest challenge while working for him was in just keeping up with him! I was more often than not the first in and the last one out of the office, because that's what it took to handle his workload—and I was just one of several support staff!

Howard was unstinting in his appreciation of my job performance, and pushed me to assume more and more responsibility. It was he who pointed me toward William Morris's new Music Department when it was created. He saw farther than others at the agency, and knew that move would offer me the fastest track toward my goal.

He was a terrific teacher, and made it clear that he was always available to me for advice and guidance, both professional and personal. Our relationship quickly advanced past mentor/employee to more like father/son. In fact, both Howard and his wife Marie practically adopted me! They welcomed me into their home on many occasions, warmly accepting and encouraging me. We stayed in touch long after I left William Morris. I still keep up with Marie, now a beautiful, dynamic lady in her eighties.

Later, during the darkest days of my lawsuit with Famous Amos over the use of my own name, Howard was among the first to offer characteristically generous support. I had written a letter to friends and colleagues asking for donations to the Wally Amos Defense Fund. I had sent one to Howard, unaware that he was in the terminal stages of heart failure. Back came a check for $500 and the following note. (Marie told me sometime later that at the time he wrote this he could barely breathe):

I have been somewhat sick recently, and may not last till the outcome [of the lawsuit] is known. But if so, I promise you that the third angel on the left, sitting in the back of the jury box will be sending you all his good wishes and prayers.

I still have that note. I treasure it. My third book, Man With No Name—the story of that legal battle—is dedicated as follows: ". . . to the memory of Howard Hausman, who demonstrated to me the meaning of friendship."

Cook's Note: When you are blessed with a mentor like Howard Hausman, do all you can to stay connected. Even after you are cooking solo in your own kitchen, breathing the air of someone really special can only improve your work.

Chocolate Chip Cookie Rock 'n' Roll

This story's for those of you who like to listen to music while you're cooking in your kitchen. It's something that dates back to my days at the William Morris Agency.

There was an unusual song that came out in the 1970s, back when I was an agent in the Music Department at William Morris. The song was "That's Good— No, That's Bad!" from a rock 'n' roll group called Sam the Sham and the Pharaohs. Basically, it's a guy telling a long story about an experience he's just had—a very complicated adventure full of ups and downs. Every time he describes what sounds like a downturn, the group he's telling the story to choruses, "Oh, that's bad!" to which he replies, "No, that's good!" and proceeds to tell how what sounded like bad luck actually positioned him for something terrific that he had been unable to foresee. When this upturn is described, the listeners chime in, "Oh, that's good!" only to be corrected with "No, that's *bad,"* and the singer then tells of the disaster that was set in motion by what first looked like a lucky break.

That song is basically the road map of my life! Until I embraced the concept of the Greater Plan that is at work in my life—God's plan, of which I am simply a tiny part—I was just like the chorus in that song, taking events at face value and thinking when I was riding high, I was in control and everything was great; and when it seemed I was as low as I could go, things were terrible and never going to get any better. Fact is, in retrospect, the times in my life I felt most in control were really the times when my life was most *out* of control. The so-called low points were actually where my most valuable lessons were waiting for me—lessons I had to grow through before moving forward and upward again.

We learn so much more from our failures than from our successes. The point is to bounce back, not roll over. The most surefire way to lose is to pull out of the game. If you just stay in play, you'll discover Life offers you infinite opportunities to win. The traditional pessimist/optimist comparison can be taken a big step farther: It's never a question of the proverbial glass being half-empty or half-full, because the truth of the Abundant Universe is that the glass is always overflowing!

Cook's Note: When you fold your basic ingredients together, expect lumps . . . but whether a lump is flour or sugar, it's still part of the batter of Life!

Ingredient Substitution:

Self-sufficiency is one of the qualities most admired in our culture, and asking for help is often looked upon as an admission of weakness. But there are times when you've done all you can do, fought the good fight, utterly exhausted your resources, and still come up short. At times like these, there's no place for false pride, and asking for help is absolutely acceptable. This next recipe is about just such a situation.

By the way, you want to live your life in such a way that the friend(s) you turn to know that you would do the same for them, if the situation were reversed!

After six-and-a-half years as a successful agent in the Music Department of the William Morris Agency, I was told that my request to be promoted to a position in either the Film or Television departments was denied. The reason given was that the powers that be at the agency felt that executives at film and TV studios were just not ready to do business with a black agent. I then suggested that my track record in Music at least warranted my being promoted to head that department. I was told no, because the other guys in the department—people I had trained—would not be willing to take direction from a black superior!

That was it. When I smacked into the race roadblock, I immediately started thinking in terms of going into business on my own. I saw the opportunity I needed with a brilliant black

South African trumpet player named Hugh Masakela, whom I'd recently signed to the agency. My path was clear! Thanks to my career at the agency, I was sure I had what it would take to promote Masakela brilliantly and create a superstar. I would leave William Morris and move lock, stock, and barrel to Los Angeles, where I would team up with others to build a self-contained music-oriented entertainment company that handled recording, music publishing, and personal talent management.

I was confident Masakela's career would bankroll our dream. I poured money into start-up costs, investing heavily in what I was sure would be a brilliant future. We made the move to the West Coast, and I fell in love with L.A.—the epicenter of the entertainment world. I was like a kid in a candy store! I was so wrapped up in my plans that I'd failed to notice the strain the move had placed on my second wife, Shirlee, who had just given birth to our son Shawn. She collapsed with a nervous breakdown.

That day is forged into my memory. I signed Shirlee into the hospital and returned home to figure out how to care for an infant and still be able to give Masakela's career the attention it needed, when the phone rang. It was Hugh Masakela, saying he was back from his tour and wanted to meet with me right away.

I had every reason to look forward to that meeting. His tour promoting our current release, "Up, Up and Away" had been a terrific success, and the song was shaping up to be a hit. There were a whole lot of neat things in motion for him that I was eager to discuss. As you can imagine, I was just about knocked flat when he arrived and announced that he wanted to terminate our business relationship. He said he was "dissatisfied" over the way I was managing his career. Bang. Just like that, the bottom dropped out of my dreams for our future. The mainstay of my new enterprise in Los Angeles had just snapped. What to do? Where to turn? I had lots of debts, a sick wife, a new baby, and my cupboard was bare.

Thank God for my friend John Levy! He was one of the top talent managers in the business. He handled entertainment heavyweights like Nancy Wilson, Cannonball Adderley, Joe Williams, and Wes Montgomery, just to name a few of his celebrity clients. Before Masakela dropped his bomb, John had offered me a job with his personal management firm. I had been riding high with my own plans and expectations at the time, so I'd turned him down. Now I had to turn around and call him to see if his offer was still good. It was, and I went to work with John's company until I was able to regroup and get my own career back on track.

Cook's Note: This is an example of a batter that appeared doomed to failure because of the disappearance of a critical ingredient. Fortunately, I was able to run next door and borrow a cup of *Support* from a friend who knew I'd have done the same for him. The end result may not have been what I'd hoped for, but at least I still had something to put on the table!

4

First Courses:

Famous Amos Start-up

My Degree from the Institute of the Cookie: M.C.S.

"Common sense is not a simple thing. Instead, it is an immense society of hard-earned practical ideas—of multitudes of life-learned rules and exceptions, dispositions, and tendencies, balances and checks."

—*Marvin Minsky*

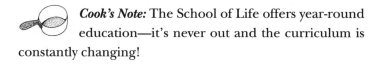 Experience is the only school that teaches Common Sense, and the curriculum to acquire it is mighty tough. Unlike conventional schooling, you are tested every day, and the results are real-life consequences. Every single experience you have is a lesson, and if you don't learn the lesson, you flunk. If you flunk, you have to face the same lesson over and over again until you master it. Only then, with that lesson under your belt, can you move on to the next level.

The "degree" I have earned as a result of my experiences with The Cookie is my M.C.S.—Master's in Common Sense. And I'd put it up against any any other academic accolade there is! As you'll see, it was quite a matriculation!

Cook's Note: The School of Life offers year-round education—it's never out and the curriculum is constantly changing!

About Dough

How many times have you thought about something you wanted to do, and then shaken your head and backed away from it, saying, "I just don't know how to do that"? People often use the adage, "Fools rush in where angels fear to tread," as an excuse not to pursue a goal. Well, in my case, "fool" or not, I got an enterprise up and running even though my naïve approach may have left a lot of "angels" shaking their heads!

When Famous Amos was launched, my dream was to create the first company ever dedicated to making and selling gourmet chocolate chip cookies. I put a proposal together not knowing that the professional term for such a document was "business plan." I called it a "proposal" because I didn't know any better. I had never opened a retail store before, so this was definitely virgin territory, but that certainly didn't stop me!

In my proposal, I attempted to show what I was going to do, how it would be done, why it was being done, and how much money it was going to cost to do it. I estimated that $25,000 was needed to launch Famous Amos, from remodeling the building, equipping the kitchen, buying ingredients, right up to pulling off a grand gala opening of my store. See, I thought all I had to do was get the store open and start selling lots of chocolate chip cookies to be able to keep going. Like I said, I'd never done anything like this before.

I have to tell you a little more about that first proposal sent out to potential backers. On the front cover there was a picture of The Famous Amos Chocolate Chip Cookie, and then attached to the inside was a little plastic bag with three cookies inside—one chocolate chip cookie with pecans, one butterscotch chip cookie with pecans, and one peanut butter chocolate chip cookie—stapled right there on the front page of the proposal. The message was, before you even turn the page, taste the cookies. If I were asking for money to launch a project involving cookies—cookies that I claimed were the best-tasting cookies ever—well, the product had better speak for itself. Then I spelled out my plans, and at the end of the proposal, I had three more cookies in a plastic bag stapled to the last page, to remind people of what they'd just read about. You see I believed in The Cookie strongly enough to put it on the line, right from the start.

Two of the first recipients of this original document were Helen Reddy and her husband at the time, Jeff Wald. Now, they were already good friends of mine—I'd known Helen from my show-business days, even before she'd become famous. They lived about ten minutes away from me, our kids played together, and they knew and loved my cookies. In fact, Jeff especially loved the dough! If I was baking up a batch of cookies at home, I'd give Jeff a call and he'd come flying down the hill to eat some cookie dough. God bless them, they agreed to put up $10,000. That left $15,000 standing between me and my goal.

Then I approached Jerry Moss, the "M" in A&M Records, who said that he would put up $5,000, and that he would get Herb Alpert, (the "A") to put up $5,000. So that was $20,000 that my unconventional proposal had produced. Now I needed only that last $5,000.

There was another record executive, a friend, named Artie Mogull who I figured might have some disposable income, so I got in touch with Artie, and sure enough, he agreed to put up $5,000. I had my $25,000! Now all I had to do was collect it, and this would prove easier said than done. But at that point, my backers were in line, and this assurance helped in getting a businessman named Bud Barrish to agree to lease me the location I had picked out.

So you see, my approach may have been naïve and unconventional, but my faith in my product is what came through that proposal, and convinced those people to believe in it as well.

Cook's Note: Dare to try unusual recipes, and include liberal doses of *Originality* . . . but when assembling your dough, be very clear about exactly what it is you need to be able to create your product, and how much.

Serendipity Soufflé:

All through my life, experience has taught me never to take any-thing at face value. Situations that seem ideal can prove disas-trous in a heartbeat; and by the same token, what appears to be a rotten piece of luck can actually open doors that lead to unexpected opportunities! Here's a recipe for a perfect case in point.

When I was looking for a place to open my first Famous Amos cookie store, I found what appeared to be a terrific location in Hollywood—right on the cor-ner of Sweetzer Avenue and Santa Monica Boulevard. The landlord was a gentleman who owned a laundry—Holloway Cleaners. It was right on Santa Monica, a beautifully busy thor-oughfare location, about three or four hundred square feet, which was exactly what I needed to get started. The owner was asking $375 a month for rent. Now understand, I didn't have any money for this enterprise yet, but I knew that this was the location I wanted: so to nail down the deal, I borrowed $750 from my friend Jay Tarses—then a producer at Mary Tyler Moore Productions—and paid the first and last months' rent. This sounds crazy, I know, but I was so sure my idea was going to work, that I went ahead without even having drawn up a business plan! Actually, I don't know who was crazier, Jay or me. In any event, the place was mine, and I was ready to roll. Or so I thought.

Just after I signed the lease, along came a county supervisor who was scouting around for an office in West Hollywood. He took one look at my location and decided he wanted it for himself. There was a signed lease, so it was technically my location. But this guy was a politician and could have made it very uncomfortable for the owner. So the owner called and told me that he was going to have to acquiesce to the county supervisor. He said he was sorry about it, though; and, as I remember it, agreed to give me about $500 worth of free laundry. That was the best I was going to get out of the deal. Great!

You're probably thinking that this doesn't sound like a very auspicious start. But actually, by this point I wanted to get out of that location! I had found a more suitable space. Where that first space was part of another building, this new place was a freestanding building on a corner in a much more heavily traveled area, smack-dab on Sunset Boulevard. It was also a much larger space—1,400 square feet! Of course, the rent was substantially more, but hey, I figured, better place, I'd sell more cookies and be able to afford higher rent! So the long and short of it was that I was looking for a way to get out of the deal, and what appeared to everyone else to be a major setback right at the outset of my enterprise was actually a terrific boost to my launching Famous Amos in the right place. That location, 7181 Sunset Boulevard, on the corner of Formosa Avenue, was to be the perfect home for The Cookie and me. The circumstances were completely out of my control; I was simply in the right place at the right time.

This is an example of what I have found to be true over and over again: Life is never what you expect it to be, it is always more!

On September 26, 2000, that corner was rechristened Famous Amos Square! How do you like those cookies?

Recipe for Serendipity Soufflé

Start with a bowl full of *Focus*—know exactly what it is you want to accomplish.

Add a generous cup each of *Faith, Commitment,* and *Vision*—stirring these three ingredients together, then mixing them with the first ingredient to bind and strengthen the dough.

When most of the lumps are smoothed out, add a generous pinch of *Serendipity* to give this dish its signature flavor and lightness. With *Serendipity,* whatever happens, even if it's not what you expected when you started out, you can be sure you'll be delighted with what you come up with.

Very important to finish this dish with a healthy sprinkling of *Acceptance* and *Receiving,* as you must be open to the ways in which *Serendipity* shapes your plan.

Cook's Note: Be prepared—this recipe comes out differently almost every time you try it.

Collaboration, not Competition

I was talking with one of my sons the other day, and during the course of the conversation he remarked that he "played to win." I thought about that for a moment, and then asked him, "What is the prize if you win?" That made us both stop and think about the concept of "*playing to win.*"

I said I thought the idea of "playing to *enjoy*" was healthier in the long run, and certainly a lot more fun than viewing everything in terms of competition. At the least, we should play to play and have fun as we go about our business—after all, satisfaction comes from the act of doing, not solely from the end result.

Life shouldn't be lived like a sporting event where you win at the expense of others, who must then by definition be "losers." We are not in competition with those around us for our space in this universe of abundance. Life is much more fun if you live it in the spirit of play and collaboration, working with instead of against others.

Cook's Note: If you find you're trying to decide between flying towards the finish line, or stopping to enjoy the view along the way, take a moment to examine that choice. The answer's pretty clear when you think about it.

Neighborhood Nutrition:

NO SUCH THING AS A "BAD LUCK" CORNER

Shakespeare's Hamlet says, "There is nothing either good or bad, but thinking makes it so." This is so true in terms of the way we tend to passively accept the judgments of others about the elements in our lives, be they objects, places, or relationships. The fact is, it's our perception *of the things around us that endows them with positive or negative values. "Good" or "Bad"? It all depends on your point of view! Here's a recipe that proves it:*

I was blessed with the most fantastic location for my first Famous Amos store—right on the corner of Sunset Boulevard and Formosa Avenue! Before committing to the lease, however, I researched the history of the location and learned that this property had started out as a House of Pies.

At one point, there was no such thing as House of Pies in Los Angeles; and then—overnight—there was a House of Pies everywhere you looked, I mean, you couldn't go around a corner in the L.A. area without bumping into one. Then, as quickly as they'd sprung up, they folded. The franchise went bust because the concept just didn't catch on. Probably because it takes a lot more fuss to eat a piece of pie than it does an ice-cream cone—or a cookie!

In any event, this location went from being a House of Pies, to a hamburger joint, to a hot-dog stand, to a car-leasing place, and by the time I had my eye on it, it had become a pinball parlor. I used to go by that place every day. I'd look at it and look at it, and I'd say to myself, "You know, this location is meant to be a cookie place! It's too great a place to be a pinball parlor—it's just being wasted!" It was downright torture to see such misuse of that wonderful place. You could even say it was "space abuse."

Finally, when I could stand it no longer, I asked my assistant, Ellen, to go in and see what was happening with the pinball place: who was leasing it from whom, and what they were up to. The day she went to check on it, the guys who were renting it were in the process of leaving. To be more accurate, they were running out on their lease! But before they vanished, Ellen managed to get the name and phone number of their landlord—a gentleman named Bud Barrish who owned a car dealership in Los Angeles—and then they were gone. We had to break the news to Bud Barrish that his tenants had split, along with the rent! For the record, another black eye for that location.

I was thrilled! There was no question this was the spot for me, and I was willing to go way out on a limb to get it. Everybody who knew me and knew what I was up to begged me not to go through with the deal. They all thought the location was a lousy risk because it had housed so many different businesses, all of which had failed ignominiously. Everybody told me it was a Bad Luck Corner.

And I said, "Come on! What can a corner possibly do to be 'bad luck'? How does a corner become bad luck? I mean, look, hundreds of thousands of cars go by here every day!"

It was so clear to me that this was a great location—after all, it was Sunset Strip! I argued that it was just that the corner had never had the right business there. It had never been presented properly. It's never been spruced up, made to look beautiful and appealing. To me it was like making sure a talented performer has just the right image in order to succeed: great presentation—a Look! I said, "That's what the corner needs, and that's what Famous Amos can bring to it."

I went to meet with Bud to convince him of my entrepreneurial viability. My intention was to put my cards squarely on the table and persuade him somehow that despite the fact that I had zero dollars in my bank account, no business plan, and no experience whatsoever in opening and operating a retail store, it was nonetheless a good risk for him to let me take over the lease for the corner property at 7181 Sunset Boulevard—the building that I had fallen in love with—for the express purpose of starting my chocolate chip cookie enterprise. My work was cut out for me, and it looked like an uphill climb. I never once doubted my vision, but I had to get him to share it.

Well, I sat with him for the longest time explaining what I had in mind. I was so passionate, so enthusiastic, so committed to my dream—so determined to make it a success! And he saw that fire in me, and God bless him, he agreed to lease the property to me. I'm sure it didn't hurt that at that time I did have backing commitments from Herb Alpert and Jerry Moss of A&M Records, and from Helen Reddy and her then-husband Jeff Wald. What I couldn't foresee was that Herb and Jerry would drop out at a critical moment later, but that's another story.

So, that is how I came to be the proud proprietor of that fantastic first home of Famous Amos. And you know what? Just as I had imagined it, believed in it and worked for it, that location turned out to be a very Good Luck Corner, indeed! The rest, as they say, is history.

Recipe for the 7181 Special

Roll up sleeves and prepare for hard work:

Start with a large dollop of *Vision*—see clearly what it is you want to accomplish.

Leaven the *Vision* with a generous cup each of *Honesty* and *Integrity*—anything less will thoroughly compromise the recipe, and result in an inferior product. In fact, short-changing either of these two crucial ingredients often results in the complete collapse of the recipe.

Stir in 1 heaping cupful of *Enthusiasm*

1½ cups of *Commitment*

1 generous tablespoon of *Passion*

Add a cup of very strong *Faith*, stirring thoroughly. This last ingredient ensures the future of the dish.

Garnish with *Congeniality*, and enjoy the "good luck" you have created!

Humble Pie 4:

KNOW WHEN TO FISH AND WHEN TO CUT BAIT

Self-sufficiency and Thrift are two terrific Entrepreneurial Extracts for your Personal Pantry. Yet, here's a recipe in which they would have really messed up the outcome—you have to use Judgment when selecting your ingredients!

The building I settled on for my very first Famous Amos cookie was a dream location—right on the very heavily traveled corner of Sunset Boulevard and Formosa Avenue. Wow, what a terrific opportunity that situation presented! The only problem was that the building itself needed a *lot* of work to live up to my lofty plans.

One of the first things I had to attend to was the storage area. The building was about 1,400 square feet, and the storeroom was a very large space in need of much repair. To begin with, there was a dusty old concrete floor that had to be cleaned up, and tile had to be laid to bring it up to health-code standards. Well, as I was on a *really* tight budget, and looking to be frugal and save wherever possible, so I figured I'd lay the tile myself. I thought, how hard can it be to glue a bunch of tiles to a cement surface?

I asked my friend Tony Christian for advice. He was very knowledgeable in these matters, and later actually wound up designing the interior of my store, and created the perfect look for a shop dedicated to selling nothing but chocolate chip cookies. He said, "Wally, it's a square room, so you just go to one corner and stretch a chalk line across the room into the opposite corner, and snap it. That gives you your centerline, so you know where to start to come out even." I figured, I can do that.

I certainly knew my way around cleaning storerooms, thanks to my early job experience in the supply room at Saks Fifth Avenue, so I cleaned that space right down to where I could have eaten off the floor. Then I took my chalk line, stretched it across the floor, and twanged it to make the centerline. And then I looked at the vast expanse of floor waiting to be tiled over, and said, "Wait a minute . . . I've never done this before in my life! I'm gonna start this, get halfway through, and go off-track somehow. Then I'm gonna have to bring in some guy who knows what he's doing, and pay him double—first to undo my mess, then to do it right. No way. What I need to do is call the tile guy *now*, and just have him do it."

And that's exactly what I did. I called an expert who'd been laying tile forever. He came in, laid the tile in no time, and did a beautiful job of it.

I learned a great lesson from that experience. Sure, there are times to go the do-it-yourself route to save money, but you have to be able to judge where that's appropriate and reasonable, and where it's actually a false economy. In those situations, it's cheaper in the long run to bite the bullet, admit ignorance, and bring in a professional.

Cook's Note: The most important ingredients I used in this situation were large doses each of *Reality, Judgment,* and *Decisiveness.* Under other circumstances, depending on what you're cooking up, *Self-Sufficiency, Perseverance,* and *Thrift* might be what you'd reach for; but in this case, they really would have made a hash of the project!

Perseverance Pâté

The Scottish poet Robert Burns said it best: "The best laid schemes o' mice and men, Gang aft a-gley." (goes oft awry) We've all been there: how many times have you painstakingly gotten all your ducks in a row, dotted every "i," crossed every "t," and still had things fall apart at the last moment? It happens. The key is not to get discouraged and give in to frustration, but to just keep going! Here's a recipe about just exactly that!

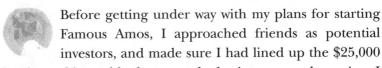Before getting under way with my plans for starting Famous Amos, I approached friends as potential investors, and made sure I had lined up the $25,000 I estimated it would take to get the business up and running. I got solid commitments from Jeff Wald and Helen Reddy, record executive Artie Mogull, Jerry Moss, and Herb Alpert (A&M Records!). All reliable individuals and solid supporters. With that money lined up, I went forward full-tilt.

As I found out, it was all well and good to have assurances from my backer friends, but things just didn't go as planned when the time came for me to collect the checks! First I went to Jeff Wald's office—Jeff and Helen had pledged $10,000.

But Jeff's business manager, Ed Gross, did not think this investment was a good idea, so the day I went to pick up the check from him, the guy had me sit in the waiting room outside his office. And sit. I sat there all morning. See, I knew Jeff had told him to draw up the check, so sooner or later he was going to have to come out and give it to me. I had nothing else to do and nowhere else to go, and I certainly wasn't going to leave without that $10,000! So, I just sat there until he finally came out and gave me the check.

As a matter of fact, during that period of my life, my heels were cooled in a number of waiting rooms, and while it was both irritating and time consuming, I could certainly understand why. A lot of the people being approached as investors were important people high up in the entertainment industry. They had a lot on their plates, and back then I was definitely low man on the food chain as far as they were concerned. While patience has never been one of my natural endowments, I certainly learned the value of practicing it. It paid off, too—I had my first $10,000 and I was on my way! I started remodeling the place and set the opening date for March 3, 1975.

By the way, when people ask me, "Wally, any particular reason you picked that date?" I tell them the date itself didn't matter anywhere near as much as the fact that one was picked, I stuck to it, focused on it, and worked toward it. I figured I needed to set an arbitrary deadline like that to put pressure on myself and make sure I stayed on task to accomplish my goal. With all that had to be done, I ran through that first $10,000 very quickly.

By now it was already February. I'd spent Jeff and Helen's money and had used up most of the $5,000 Artie Mogull had put up. With March 3 rushing toward me, and close to zero dollars in the bank again, it felt like it was time to contact Jerry Moss and Herb Alpert, who'd been on vacation and out of reach. I really needed the $5,000 they'd each said they'd commit in order to finish the remodeling and be able to go into full operation in time for Opening Day.

So about a month before my original Opening Day deadline, I called Jerry Moss, and to my dismay he said, "You know, Wally, I'm just not going to be able to do it. Herb and I are kind of overextended." Now, this was a man who was worth millions of dollars! I mean, A&M Records was one of the most successful record companies ever. To him, $5,000 was pocket change—chicken feed. He wasn't "overextended," he was undercommitted. He had simply changed his mind. I heard that in the tone of his voice. I knew I could have talked with him forever, and his decision would have remained firm. I had to accept that as gracefully as I could, and turn my attention to getting the money from some other source as quickly as possible. (By the way, I harbored absolutely no ill feelings whatsoever toward Jerry and Herb at the time, and later on A&M wound up donating quite a lot of valuable support in terms of graphic design and marketing materials.)

When I hung up the phone after that setback, I walked into the little cubicle that was my office, and got out my phone book. I started looking through that directory for a name that just might have $10,000 next to it. The name I stopped at was Marvin Gaye.

Now, this is an interesting story: I placed a call to Marvin, who was out, so I left a message. Then, while I was waiting in the reception area of the president of Universal Pictures—Ned Tannen, a man I'd known for years—my assistant, Ellen, called to let me know that Marvin Gaye had returned my call and wanted me to get back to him. I called him from that waiting room, got him on the line, and started right in describing what it was I was up to with The Cookie and Famous Amos, and my store and all.

He stopped me in mid-pitch and said, "Wally, Wally . . . hey, wait a minute, man. If you're doin' it, that's OK, I'll invest in it." And just like that, he was in for the $10,000 I needed! My shortfall set me back only a week, and thanks to Marvin, my plans were back on track, with Famous Amos now set to open on March 10, 1975.

Recipe for Perseverance Pâté

Some recipes are more challenging than others! In the situation I've just described, even though I thought I had my ingredients all lined up, they seemed to slip right through my fingers! Should this happen to you, reach immediately for a pound of *Tenacity* (common name: *Stick-to-it-iveness*) and mix with *Patience* and *Forbearance.* If an ingredient is going to disappear on you, don't waste your energy losing your temper! That doesn't get you anywhere, and your mood actively drives people away from your kitchen. Add a large dash each of *Acceptance* and *Adaptability,* so that when circumstances force you to alter your recipe, you're flexible enough to do so successfully. Keep adding ample measures of *Faith* in what you want to accomplish, even in the face of unexpected setbacks and loss. Use *Energy* and strong *Focus* to blend these ingredients into a smooth consistency. Garnish this dish with strong *Credibility.* People will always come back to the table of a chef they know they can count on.

A Treat from the Garden

Cooking and gardening have a lot in common. Both involve planning, working with your hands, and creating something that others can enjoy. This recipe comes from an experience I had while taking a break from the kitchen.

 I recently had the chance to spend some time in our garden, doing some long-overdue pruning. There was a wild-looking tree that had grown out of control. I cut it back pretty drastically—in fact, so much so that when I finished, I worried that I'd been a little overzealous. The truth is, I thought I'd killed it.

I checked on that tree a week later, and every available knob on the lower branches was covered with tiny new shoots poised to sprout! Now, those branches had been barren when I pruned the tree just seven days before.

Think about the lesson here! Life is absolutely indomitable! That tree really did look dead when I'd finished with it, but within a week, the life force within it had gathered and prepared to sprout anew. Think about those tiny, delicate growths pushing inexorably through the tough exterior of those thick lower branches—nothing was going to stop them. Think also about the metaphor of pruning—the traumatic cutting back actually stimulated that tree to produce new growth!

It's not much of a stretch to draw the comparison between that tree and what happens to us when we encounter adversity in our lives. It doesn't have to defeat us! It can pave the way for new growth! To go back to our culinary premise: The Cookie *never* crumbles!

Recipe for "Gardener's Delight"

This is a recipe you reach for when challenged by adversity.

Start with a large measure of *Acceptance.* You can't change what's happened, so don't waste precious energy fighting it.

Add a large cup each of *Courage, Stick-to-it-iveness, Determination, Indefatigability, Tenacity,* and *Resourcefulness.*

Top off with a large measure of *Faith* in God's plan, and the life force within you.

Combine ingredients, and focus your attention on answers and solutions. You'll be astonished at the options that appear to you. Remember: You cannot be defeated if you refuse to admit defeat!

Humble Pie 14:

KNOWING WHEN TO CALL IN THE CAVALRY

The famous architect Mies van der Rohe said, "God is in the details." And is that ever true! When I was in the process of shifting over from baking my chocolate chip cookies at home to producing them on a commercial scale, I discovered I had a lot to learn in order to get the details absolutely right. Over and over again I was blessed by fortuitously getting hooked up with the right people just in the nick of time. This recipe is all about one gentleman who saved Famous Amos from near disaster right at the outset!

I made cookies at home for years. Obviously, I had an oven and a refrigerator where the ingredients were stored, a ceramic mixing bowl, a wooden spoon—did not have an electric mixer; had a little table—actually, a sink counter—that I worked on.

When I went commercial with The Cookie, however, my domestic facilities were woefully inadequate. I needed a big mixer, a bigger refrigerator, a bigger oven. I needed baker's scales because my little old measuring cup wasn't going to be up to the job. In short, I needed all kinds of basic equipment to go from at-home cookie baking to baking industrial-sized batches of them.

I didn't have a clue where to turn, so I went to the Yellow Pages to start looking for someone who could supply me with this equipment. I was flying absolutely blind here, and I had the good fortune—the blessing—to find a guy named Clarence

Tucker who worked for a commercial kitchen-supply company. Clarence Tucker was a gentle, extremely knowledgeable, kind human being. He walked me through exactly what I needed, and what I didn't need—in other words, where I could cut corners to save money without jeopardizing the quality of my product.

He said, "Wally, you don't need all-new equipment! I'll get you a nice used mixer—the good ones are built to last; don't go for a new one. Scales, well, they don't cost that much—you should have new scales. You should have a new refrigerator, too, because you don't want to buy somebody else's problem." And so on. He found me workbenches. I was fortunate enough to find a nice used stainless-steel sink, from a Chicken Delight restaurant that had gone out of business. He recommended new ovens for the same reason he'd argued for a new refrigerator, but he never had me buy a new piece of equipment where a used one would do just as well. He knew I was on a very tight budget, and he was just so resourceful in helping me gather my kitchen together.

But he didn't stop at that. After I'd gotten the store opened, and was mass-producing cookies, I noticed that they somehow didn't taste quite like the cookies that came out of my kitchen at home. And I wasn't the only one to notice the discrepancy, either! Now when I'd been a personal talent manager, I used to give out my homemade chocolate chip cookies at A&M all the time. I'd go around and share cookies with everyone, encouraging them to support my clients. Everybody at A&M knew and loved my cookies. One day after my store opened, a friend, named Julie, called me and whispered into the phone: "Hey, Wally . . . Wally . . . the cookies, umm, don't taste the same!!"

I told her, "Julie, I know they don't taste the same, but I'm workin' on it—don't tell anybody!"

Boy, was I skating on thin ice at the time, because obviously there were some things that weren't working right and I just didn't have the experience to know what to look for to be able to solve the problems. For example, every time my mixer would stop, the beater would disconnect and fall off into the batter. I knew that wasn't right, but had no idea how to stop that from happening. I'd always prided myself on my self-sufficient, "can-do" independent attitude, but I was at a dead loss here, and if I couldn't mass-produce home-baked quality cookies, it was going to be curtains for Famous Amos.

Finally, I swallowed my pride and called Clarence. I described the problem and he came right over. Bless his heart, he knew exactly what to do. He opened the electrical compartment on that mixer and said, "What you got here Wally, is a three-phase beater—three-phase electricity—and your wires are crossed. See, all you got to do is switch these wires . . ." Which he did. I turned the mixer on, then turned it off, and the beater stayed on! Now, I could have fussed with that mixer, and wasted a lot of time on trial and error—I might even have broken it! But Clarence had the knowledge to cut right to the chase. That's where experience is invaluable.

It didn't stop there, either. While he was with me, I wanted to mix up some batter, so I began weighing out ingredients on the scale he'd found for me. You know how that works: You put the weights you need on one side of the scale, and then you add the ingredients to the other side till the two sides balance. Clarence watched me for a moment, and then said very gently, "Wally, I think I know what's happening with your cookies." As it turned out, I had the sides of the scales reversed! As a result, I'd been using way too much flour in my batter—no wonder my cookies didn't taste the same as they did at home! The other measurements were off as well, but the flour mismeasurement was the main offender.

So that's two ways in that one visit Clarence saved the day!

Thanks to him, I was able to get my cookies looking and tasting like the ones I'd known and loved for so long. There is no telling what would have happened to Famous Amos if I hadn't called him for help.

Cook's Note: This story offers a good example of an ingredient that should be banned from your Personal Pantry: *False Pride.* When you find yourself in a situation where you know you don't know what you're doing, find an experienced person and *ask for help*! I have been so blessed in my life! God has always led me to the right person in the nick of time. But if you don't reach for the *Humility* on your shelf, *False Pride* can cancel out the subtle flavor of His guidance.

Green Cookies

Remember the Golden Rule of Recipes in Part I: how A, B, and C ingredients combine to give you X as a result? How, if you are happy with X, you don't change A, B, or C? Well, it took a costly lesson to impress the importance of that rule upon me.

When I was brand-new to the commercial cookie industry, the very first bakery-supply company I did business with was Wesco, and the salesman who handled my account was a man named Leo. I bought all my ingredients from Leo. Leo was one of these guys that had been in the bakery business all his life. To him, I was just a babe in the woods, and he took it upon himself to show me how the pros in the bakery world went about their business.

My goal was to make the very same cookies that I had been making at home. I was adamant about that and figured the logical way to do that would be to use the exact same ingredients. A + B + C = X, right? X was the chocolate chip cookie that I loved. So when I placed my first order for ingredients with Leo, I told him I wanted to use real vanilla—not vanillin, the artificial vanilla substitute. Leo's response was, "Aww, Wally, you don't want pure vanilla extract! All the other bakeries use imitation flavoring."

That was my first clue that I needed to stick to my vision and use pure vanilla extract. I wanted to be different. My cookies would be real with a homemade taste, not imitation. It's the pure vanilla that gives them that taste! So I insisted, saying, "Why would I want to do what the other bakeries are doing if

I'm trying to create something that's different from their product?"

We got through that debate, and then it came to the chocolate chips. Now, my main ingredient here is chocolate chips— I'm talking about building a business that sells homemade chocolate chip cookies, right? At home, I'd always used genuine semisweet chocolate morsels. Leo said, "Awwwww, Wally, Wally! You don't want to do that. All the bakeries use imitation chocolate."

"No way," I said and reiterated, "I don't want to make imitation cookies with vanilla substitute and artificial chocolate, I want *real* cookies, made with the *real* ingredients I've always used!"

I had to fight this guy every step of the way! I mean, I know he was trying to save me money, but I wanted to create a superior product. I figured if the cookies were truly superior, then people would be willing to pay more for them.

Well, we wrangled our way through the list—fortunately there wasn't much room to differ over things like brown and white sugar, or eggs. Then we came to the flour. I wanted all-purpose flour because that's what I'd always used. Leo said, "Awww, Wally, you don't want to use all-purpose flour! There's a special cookie/cake blend of flour that all the bakers use." And here's where he got me. I wanted to consider myself a baker, and if this special flour was what all the bakers were using, well, then, there must be something to it.

I had Leo send me that so-called special flour, and it *totally* ruined my cookies! It turned them green! It made them hard— they were just plain inedible. I got Leo on the phone and told him exactly what I thought of his "special cookie/cake blend," and that he was to get me some all-purpose flour ASAP!

I learned a couple of lessons the hard way here. First, as I've said, if the formula is successful—*don't mess with it!* Second,

don't let people talk you out of what you know you want—
stick to it.

Recipe

Start with hearty helpings each of *Confidence* and *Commitment*: When you know what you want, believe in your choices. Add a cup of *Decisiveness*: No waffling about presenting what you want. Complete the recipe with a good measure of *Tenacity*, and don't let anyone talk you out of what you want!

Cook's Note: *on Successful Recipes,* "If it ain't broke, don't fix it!"

Caddie Woodlawn's Recipe Redux

As the national spokesperson for Literacy Volunteers of America, it just tickles me to be able to link this recipe to the wonderful children's classic by Carol Ryrie Brink!

During the course of preparing to launch the Famous Amos Company, I was working on the graphics and art design for my Famous Amos Cookie bags. I had arranged for a photo shoot with my friend David Alexander, a terrific professional photographer I'd met during the course of my work in the entertainment industry.

We agreed on a day, and he told me to come with a bunch of different outfits—clothes I felt comfortable in. He said that way he'd be able to give me a number of options to choose from. Sounded good to me . . .

So I showed up with the clothes, and we shot and shot and shot! I don't know how many times I changed clothes. (With each "look," though, I kept the same panama hat.) It took an entire day, but it was time well invested. I left the session confident that out of the hundreds of pictures we'd taken, there would be at least one that would capture the essence of what I was launching and jump out at us as The Perfect Picture.

Well, time passed, and finally David sent me the proofs from our session. *Aughhhhhhhhh!* To my dismay, he'd done something wrong with the lighting and I came out incredibly dark! All you could make out clearly in each shot were my teeth. Obviously, this just wouldn't do.

I had a choice. I could jump up and down and storm about

the time wasted—time that I didn't have to spend. By now it was December. Not only did I not have time to redo the day's shoot, but at that point I was running around trying to conquer massive financial problems as well. I certainly could have pitched a hissy fit. But where would that have gotten me? Fact was, it hadn't worked the first time. If I wanted to have a decent picture for my cookie bag design, I was going to have to bite the bullet and haul myself into another photo session with David Alexander. Period. And that's just what I did.

The result of that session was *the* famous "Famous Amos" photograph: me in my panama hat and Indian gauze shirt, holding up my right index finger with a conspiratorial twinkle in my eyes as I grinned up at where the image of the cookie would be superimposed later. That wonderful picture would never have come to pass if we hadn't gone ahead with the retake.

So what, you ask yourself, does this story have to do with *Caddie Woodlawn*? I'll tell you. There's a chapter in that book that offers the classic bromide: "If at first you don't succeed, try, try again." Now, anyone who knows me at all is just waiting for what they know is coming! I am dead set against "try" and emphasize over and over again the importance of *"Do!"* "Try" is feeble, where positive action is needed to accomplish a goal. And, as my book is a cookbook, it would be nice to express the lesson in culinary terms, so I much prefer the way the heroine in Carol Ryrie Brink's classic puts it.

Caddie's Counsel "If at first you can't fricassee, fry, fry a hen!" In other words, once you've targeted the problem, you have no other logical recourse but to do whatever it takes to remedy the situation.

Magic with Margarine:

OR, HOW NEAR-DISASTER GREASED THE WAY

This recipe is another example of how what looks like a disaster in the making can actually be a necessary step on the way to an unexpected opportunity. The lesson is to never panic when it looks like a situation is turning sour—stay with it, ride it and keep your eyes open to how it can be turned to your advantage!

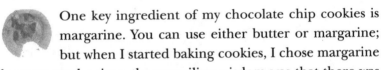 One key ingredient of my chocolate chip cookies is margarine. You can use either butter or margarine; but when I started baking cookies, I chose margarine because, at the time, the prevailing wisdom was that there was some health benefit to using margarine over butter. Now that's come into question, but back then I went with margarine. I'd always gotten great-tasting cookies using it, and I certainly wanted to sell the same cookies in my store that I'd made at home. Plus, it was cheaper than butter; so when I went commercial with my cookies, I figured if margarine was both more economical and more healthful than butter, well, it was kind of a no-brainer choice!

I bought my margarine from a bakery supply house called Wesco, the company that had been providing all my ingredients for Famous Amos Cookies since I'd opened. They packaged their margarine in huge thirty-pound tin tubs. I needed five pounds of margarine for each batter, so I'd have to take a scraper, scoop out the margarine and measure it on the scale. If I was going to make ten batters, then I'd have to measure out ten five-pound scoops of margarine so I could get my little assembly-line production going. It was a very, very cumbersome, messy process.

By now I was getting behind in my bills—see, I was naïvely operating under the assumption that all I had to do to stay in business was sell a lot of cookies. I had had backers to help me get my store opened and launch Famous Amos, but there was still no one on the financial front at this point investing additional money to keep me going.

One day, without any warning, Wesco stopped sending me margarine. They simply said, "We can't do it, Wally, because you've got an outstanding balance here, and unless you give us some money, we can't send you margarine." But I didn't have any money to pay them right then because cash was really tight. It was pretty clear that that was the line they were going to take on the other ingredients they'd been supplying me with, too.

Things looked pretty bleak for Famous Amos and The Cookie. But thank goodness a gentleman named Bob Belton of Continental Food Service really wanted my business! He would come around from time to time just to say hello and see how everything was going, and during that period he and I had developed a nice friendship. (Remember: Friendship is one of our "Relationship Relishes," and it certainly came in handy here!)

So there I was. I couldn't get margarine, and without margarine, I couldn't bake cookies. So I called up Bob Belton, and after a little small talk, I said, "You know, Bob, you've been trying your darnedest to do some business with me, and maybe there's an opportunity here. What's your price on margarine?"

Not only was his price cheaper than what I'd been paying for Wesco's margarine, but his margarine came in thirty-pound units of individually wrapped one-pound cubes—no more sloppy scooping! Using his product really streamlined my production process!

Bob Belton believed in Famous Amos and The Cookie. He put his money where his mouth was, too. He opened a line of credit for me so I could buy my ingredients from him and keep on baking cookies to be able to meet my bills. It was a pleasure to do business with him. Our friendship, his faith in my product, and his margarine kept Famous Amos from slip-sliding away in those challenging early days.

Recipe for Saving a Sticky Situation

(I have to credit Bob Belton here. This is one he taught me.)

Establish a healthy *Friendship* based on shared interests.

Season with *Respect* and strengthen with *Communication*.

Watch the mixture closely to spot the perfect moment to add a dash of *Opportunity*.

Carefully blend in one heaping cup each of *Generosity* and *Trust*.

Keep the cookies from getting stuck by liberally greasing the situation with margarine.

Cook's Note: My addition to this recipe is *Faith*—I countered the taste of fear in this precarious situation with a healthy dose of my own strong *Faith* that it would work out for the best. And, as always happens, the result wasn't what I'd expected—it was more!

A Helping of Hana Hou

"Hana hou" is Hawaiian for "encore," or "do it again." Usually it's an expression of encouragement for a successful performance, but that was not the case in this instance!

When I started Famous Amos, I had that wonderful photograph taken of me in my West Indian shirt and panama hat, smiling and pointing up at a giant Cookie. It was such a great picture that I decided to use it for my Famous Amos PR posters.

I called my friend Phil Jaffe, who was a rep for a printing company, and placed an order for posters to be printed up from our finished art. This was a big investment for me at that time, as I was literally on a shoestring budget, but I figured that money spent on PR was a necessary investment.

Well, the posters came in, hundreds of them and, to my horror, the color was wrong. It wasn't grotesque or anything, but it was distinctly off. Those posters just weren't right. They wouldn't do. See, my criteria for evaluating anything that had to do with the Famous Amos Company was that it had to be on a par with the quality of The Cookie. Period. I figured that if I was offering the world the *best* chocolate chip cookie ever, then everything surrounding that product had to be of commensurate quality. Anything less would diminish The Cookie, and cost me credibility in the marketplace.

So I called Phil—who is, by the way, a neat guy. I told him he was going to have to take the posters back and redo them. Of course, this was not something he wanted to hear. We went back and forth for a while, but ultimately he had to admit I was right. He redid the entire order, and I wound up throwing that first batch out. I hated to do it—hated to kill more trees, hated to waste the paper, hated to make Phil swallow the cost of those posters. But anything less would have wound up being more expensive in the long run.

That was a big lesson for me: had I settled for the first batch of posters, my PR would have been much less effective in selling The Cookie, and that would have cost me. I would have been disappointed with Phil's product, and certainly wouldn't have brought my business back to him—that would have cost him. Had Phil refused to redo the posters, not only would he have lost my business, but his own estimation of himself as a professional would have been diminished—nobody feels good about letting mediocrity slide by. Plus, our friendship would have been seriously compromised. In short, it would have been a lose-lose situation all around.

As it turned out, we all wound up winners: Phil, me and The Cookie. You've got to go with what you know in your heart is right. It's just like my struggle for top-quality ingredients with Leo—the guy whose "special blend" flour turned my cookies green. You simply cannot allow someone else to dictate your standards for you. It's absolutely up to you to establish them and stand by them; and P.S.—they need to be very, very, *very* high.

Cook's Note: No matter what it is you're working on, everything that touches the product must be of the highest possible quality. *Integrity* is a key ingredient here, along with *Self-Confidence* and *Perseverance.* You must demand the best of yourself, insist on the best from others, and never settle for anything less.

Resource Ratatouille:

OR, THE LEAST EXPENSIVE/MOST CREATIVE WAY
TO GET EVERYONE INTO THE POT

Nowadays, thanks to movies with multimillion-dollar budgets, lavishly designed Broadway productions, and exorbitant business expense accounts, the message we are constantly bombarded with is the more money you spend on something, the better it must be! Well, this recipe is proof positive that that just does not have to be the case, and that ingenuity, creativity, and imagination can go a l-o-n-g way, even with extremely limited resources!

In the spring of 1975, I found myself facing a serious dilemma as the deadline for the Famous Amos store opening I'd planned drew near. I needed to generate a lot of publicity for the March 9 event, but by the time my doors opened to the public on Monday, March 10, I was going to be flat out of money. I had funds enough for only two ads that were scheduled to run on my first day of business—one in the *Hollywood Reporter,* and the same ad in the *Daily Variety.* I chose those two publications because they would get my message to everyone in the entertainment industry, who could then take my story to the general public.

Before the official opening, my idea was to throw a huge blowout party, bring in as many of the media as possible, and generate enough word of mouth to get paying customers stampeding into my store the first day. The important thing was to spread the word on Famous Amos for free! Actually, free publicity wasn't a question of what I wanted, it was what was necessitated by my financial status at the time, which was zero. But how to get the word out without spending beaucoup dollars I didn't have?

Well, because of my time in the entertainment industry—over six years as an agent with the William Morris Agency in New York, and another seven years in Los Angeles as a personal talent manager—I had contacts in all the motion-picture studios, record companies, and TV networks. I asked my friends in these media centers to send me company personnel lists. Then I addressed invitations to everyone on those lists. I boxed up the envelopes and personally delivered them to each of the companies. Because the security guards knew me from my talent management days, all I had to say to gain access was "I'm just going to see so-and-so." Then I'd give them some cookies, and in I'd go!

Once inside, I'd leave the box of invitations with the people in the mailroom—with another bag of cookies—and ask them to distribute them to the appropriate boxes. No postage! Twenty-five hundred invitations were sent that way, which saved over $325! That may not sound like much today, but it's a lot if you're broke. It was certainly a labor-intensive way to go, but I'm telling you, the investment paid off.

Party Day—Sunday, March 9—finally rolled around, and over 1,500 people showed up! The guests arrived early—a whole spectrum of people, from the friends and media moguls I'd invited, to curious passersby. Guccis, Nikes, earth shoes, and sandals crossed my threshold that day to celebrate the christening of Famous Amos and The Cookie. Out back, in the tented AstroTurf parking area, champagne and milk flowed freely as trayfuls of cookies disappeared, spreading deliciously infectious "brown fever." We had a West Indian steel-drum band, a roving jug band made up of kids who were relatives of my former land-lord, all contributing to the carnival atmosphere. The corner of Sunset Boulevard and Formosa Avenue was jammed with people coming and going. We stopped traffic on Sunset Boulevard! We had valet parking and a red carpet from the sidewalk to the entrance of the store. Other people just pulled up and parked wherever in order to get a taste of this fun in the sun, and to "have a very brown day!" with Famous Amos and The Cookie. It was just wonderful—better than I could have hoped: a monster hit and the best possible way to set the stage for Famous Amos!

In addition to being a glorious party, the event really paid off. The next morning, as we were scampering around getting everything ready to open for business, we could see people lining up to buy cookies all the way down the street! Just as I'd hoped, folks who had tasted The Cookie were sold on it, and couldn't wait to become customers. We started with a bang, and business just kept growing!

Recipe for This Rich Ratatouille

To prepare your pot, sprinkle it liberally with *Focus*: Know clearly what you want to accomplish.

If you know you're on a tight budget, take careful stock of the ingredients you have to work with—a dash of *Reality* helps here.

Toss in as many positive *Relationships* as you can gather— the more the merrier, and each contributes its own unique flavor and gift to the mix. (Remember, a good cook always maintains a wide variety of these on hand!)

Attention to Detail is a critical factor in this process.

Toss in a generous pint of *Serendipity* to enrich the stock. (The beautiful weather we had for the party certainly contributed to its astonishing success).

Don't stint on *Elbow Grease* and *Frugality*—a thrifty cook is not afraid of hard work, and if your resources are carefully managed, this recipe is a terrific dollar-stretcher.

OOPS! I almost forgot a most important ingredient: a large helping of *Fun!*

Apple Pie Order

Focus and Determination are critical ingredients, whether your goal is monumental, or as simple as pursuing a slice of pie!

One evening, after dinner with my son Gregory in New York City, I had a burning desire for some apple pie. There was none on the menu, so we moved on. I needed to purchase a book, so we visited a Barnes & Noble. I checked their café—no apple pie.

As we ambled toward my hotel, we noticed an Au Bon Pain restaurant. "Surely they'll have apple pie," I said to Gregory. Wrong!

We passed a cafeteria that surely would have apple pie, but no, plenty of different kinds of cakes, but no apple pie. We looked in at several delis along the way—No apple pie! Even in the restaurant at my hotel: No apple pie!!!

By now, my desire had grown in direct proportion to the elusiveness of my goal. I was determined to succeed in my search. I decided to walk Gregory to the subway. Across the street from the hotel was a café-restaurant that had something like apple pie with what appeared to be strange sugary icing. I asked to see it up close. It looked pretty tired, and cost $4.00 for a tiny slice—not what I had in mind. I knew what I wanted, and refused to settle for anything less!

The bakery/coffee shop in Grand Central Station was a bust as well. Even a bakery Gregory remembered in the area came up empty—some cakes, assorted tarts, but no trace of apple pie. This was getting ridiculous!

By this time, Gregory had had it with the hunt. I bade him good night, and watched him disappear into the depths of the subway station. I was left alone with my obsession. As I turned, I spotted a Starbucks ten feet ahead. I slipped in just before they closed, and there, on the bottom shelf of the pastry display rack was the most beautiful, fresh open-faced apple pie I'd ever seen. It was the pie of my dreams—just what I'd been salivating for! I bought it for the very reasonable price of $3.25. On the way back to my hotel, I ate every bit of what was to me, the most delicious apple pie in the world—all the sweeter for the chase!

Cook's Note: This may sound like a relatively trivial incident, but *Focus, Stick-to-it-iveness,* and *Determination* pay off on any scale!

Golden Nuggets

This recipe is drawn from an incident I will remember for the rest of my life, and reminds me that no matter how big an event—or sequence of events—it all still comes down to taking the time to appreciate what comes your way moment by moment.

I had planned a huge blowout party to celebrate and launch the official opening of the first Famous Amos store. As you can imagine, there were tons of things to do to prepare for the event, but because Famous Amos was as yet an unborn enterprise, there were no employees, no staff—no one but me to do them all.

Miraculously enough, things seemed to be moving along smoothly. About noon the day before the big party, the torrential rain had finally let up, the painters had just left, and I'd finally gotten all my kitchen stuff in order. We'd just squeaked under the wire in terms of getting the place ready in time, but we'd done it. Now the stage was set for the success I'd put everything on the line for. All that was left to do was to bake the cookies for the next day's celebration—thousands of cookies—and I was the only one who knew how to do it. So there I was, alone in my big new commercial kitchen, facing a l-o-n-g night of cookie baking. But the most vivid memory I have of that night is not of my fatigue or apprehension about the events of the next day. It's of when I was opening up my ingredients to put them into the big ingredient bins to start the first of many batches that night. I opened a case of pecans first.

Now, when I baked cookies at home, my recipe called for a

little bitty bag of those pecans. This was a thirty-pound box of large, golden pecan pieces. They were *so beautiful*! It was like a box of gold! I put my hands all the way down to the bottom and pulled them up and just watched the pecans trickle through my fingers. That memory is just so vivid—I can see it very very clearly to this day.

It was a wonderful moment, and I was absolutely present in the middle of it. Appreciating the joy of that moment really energized me and propelled me into the task that lay ahead of me that night.

Cook's Note: Sometimes invaluable inspiration can come from your simplest ingredients. Make sure you take the time to stop and appreciate them!

5

Entrées:

Famous Amos Full-Tilt

Fricassée du Lapin (Rabbit Stew)

This recipe is all about making choices—deciding whether to stick to a preconceived gameplan when a situation doesn't pan out, or to keep your eye on your long-range goal and realign expectations to stay on target.

Early on, I was looking for some kind of unusual vehicle to serve as my "Cookiemobile." I needed a car for delivering my cookies that would be a rolling advertisement for Famous Amos and The Cookie, catching people's eyes, making them smile and feel great as it went by. That was about the time that Volkswagen came out with the Rabbit. This was a car with a very high cuteness factor, and I decided that this was the car for The Cookie and me. I'd wanted a white model, but there were none in stock, so I wound up leasing one that was bright yellow—lemon yellow, actually. This wound up to be a prophecy of things to come. I didn't know that at the time, though, and the company that I leased the car from certainly offered no cause for concern as they handed over the keys.

So, I had this cute little Rabbit painted with the same image of me and The Cookie that was on all the bags and posters. It was painted on the side panel of the car, which, unfortunately, was so low to the ground that instead of pointing up at The Cookie, I was pointing straight out to the large Cookie at my side. I had a giant decal of The Cookie created and put on the hood, and on the back of the car was my logo and all the contact information. Then I was ready to roll with my customized little Cookiemobile.

I got an order from Macy's of San Francisco—my very first venture selling cookies outside of Los Angeles. Everything I'd done in terms of marketing The Cookie prior to that had been confined to the Los Angeles area. It was a very exciting prospect to open this account in San Francisco and break into a whole new market. This represented a tremendous growth opportunity for Famous Amos.

I'd been having some minor problems with my Rabbit, oil leaking and such, and since I was looking at a seven- or eight-hour drive to San Francisco, I wanted to make sure the car would be able to get me there safely. I took it to Bob Smith's Volkswagen dealership, asked them to service it, and double-check that everything was in good working condition. The report came back: Everything was A-OK.

On the appointed day, I loaded up my little yellow customized Cookiemobile with twenty cases of cookies—twelve one-pound bags per case, and prepared to head for San Francisco—full of entrepreneurial dreams of greener pastures. And then it happened: just outside of Modesto, California, on U.S. 5, black smoke started billowing out of the engine. I managed to get the steaming Rabbit to limp along to a pay phone, and called a VW dealer in Modesto. I wound up having to stay in Modesto overnight while they worked to try and get the Rabbit up and running again.

Now, I was due to make a big entrance at Macy's that next day. We'd lined up the media to cover Famous Amos and The Cookie roaring into San Francisco in my customized Cookiemobile. Unfortunately, given the sad state of the Rabbit, this was not going to happen. So I had a choice: either to stick to my original idea, and wait as long as it took to get my Cookiemobile back in action in order to make the flashy entrance I'd planned so carefully—in which case I'd risk losing the media coverage that had been arranged, and the "big entrance" would be for naught; *or* I could settle for less of a ta-dah entrance, and still make optimum use of the media, in addition to delivering my cookies to Macy's when I said I'd have them in the store.

When you lay it out like that, the best choice is pretty clear. I accepted another distinctly nondescript Rabbit as a loaner from the dealership in Modesto, shifted my twenty cases of cookies from the ailing Cookiemobile, and headed on into San Francisco. The cookies got into Macy's on schedule and, despite the more modest entrance, we went on to have a great promotion—got a lot of media coverage of me selling cookies in Macy's, and everything went just fine. In fact, Macy's went on to become one of my bigger national accounts—which might never have happened if I'd let that disappointing setback cause me to lose sight of my long-term goal, which was to get Famous Amos cookies into Macy's and successfully launch that business relationship.

Cook's Note: In situations like this, you simply have to accept the fact that you plan and God laughs. You must bring *Faith* into the mix, and believe that He's not laughing at you! With a cup each of *Acceptance* and *Flexibility*, you can discover how He makes it possible for you to enjoy the joke right along with Him.

East Coast Entrée

Every good cook should know how to operate on a tight budget. This recipe is all about doing whatever you have to do to make sure a dish that has been promised gets to the table, and not letting a monetary shortfall cost you an opportunity!

Barbara Dullien, a gifted dress designer, and a good customer of my first Famous Amos store on Sunset Boulevard, convinced me that *the* thing to do was to get my cookies into what was at the time, the hottest store on the planet—Bloomingdale's. Barbara had said, "You simply must be in Bloomie's!" one too many times, and had turned my head in that direction. At the time, she had a line of her apparel in Bloomingdale's, and was very well connected with the management there. She introduced me to the top executives, and it was agreed that I should bring my cookies into "Bloomie's."

What was I thinking?! I had all I could deal with just keeping my head above water with the Los Angeles store! I had no disposable capital to invest in another location, still had no outside investors backing me. Nevertheless, it became my goal to bring The Cookie into that upscale Manhattan emporium. And so I did!

There were so many hoops to jump through! Shipping cookies from the West Coast was out of the question—the airfreight costs would have killed me. The only solution was to establish an East Coast bakery to supply the new location. This meant scouting for a place, leasing it, preparing it, gathering the equipment, hiring and training the personnel. I found a great location in Nutley, New Jersey—isn't that great? A chocolate chip cookie bakery in a town called "Nutley"! I knew it was meant to be, but the Nutley City Council took a lot of convincing. Another hoop. And all the while my credit was stretching thinner and thinner as the Bloomingdale's opening date approached.

It took longer than I'd expected to get the bakery in Nutley set up, and it became very clear that it wouldn't be up and running in time. So I arranged to have cookies shipped from my stores in Los Angeles and Tucson—a large, additional unexpected expense. It solved the problem, though, and the Bloomingdale's opening was a spectacular success. I sailed through a lovely reception up in the boardroom with all of the executives present and enthusiastic. I went down and sold cookies in the store for a while, and then I had to get the hell out of there—by that time, I was $15,000 overdrawn on my personal checking account. As a result of this adventure, I was completely bankrupt!

But Famous Amos was in Bloomingdale's, at the very peak of that prestigious store's trendy popularity. That was worth a lot in terms of credibility. As it turned out, this came in very handy. I had met a guy named Stu Brown, a New York investment banker. When I left the Bloomingdale's promotion, I went straight to his office, and he arranged for me to borrow the $15,000 to cover my debts—just in the nick of time! Those were the circumstances that I was operating under for a very, very long time: running on fumes because there was no cash.

But I've never let not having money get in my way! Lack of funds is simply not a good reason not to pursue your goals. It's an excuse for not succeeding! The one thing I knew was that if I stopped, I'd be out of business. You've just got to keep going. The answer will come if you do. The one thing you can't do is quit—the only ironclad guarantee I know of is that if you quit, you will fail. If you go forward with commitment, determination, and perseverance, eventually you will succeed!

Recipe for East Coast Entrée

(This recipe calls for a good deal of *Hard Work*—a.k.a. *"Elbow Grease"*!)

Start with *Vision* accelerated with *Friendship* and *Connections*.

To this mix add a tablespoon each of *Courage, Commitment,* and *Resourcefulness.*

Balance the bubbles of *Enthusiasm* that are generated with a spritz of *Patience.*

Toss in healthy handfuls of *Credibility* and *Faith* to bring this dish to a successful completion.

Lumps

Someone recently asked me if I've ever had trouble with unions over the course of my adventures with Famous Amos. I can honestly answer that I've had very good relations with the unions I've dealt with, with one notable exception. This next recipe comes from that experience.

In 1975, we contracted to bring Famous Amos into Bloomingdale's! This was quite a coup, but in order to make it work, we found that we needed to open up a baking operation on the East Coast. We found a perfect facility in the town of Nutley, New Jersey, and set up our bakery there.

It was a nonunion operation. We were desperate to have it up and running in time for the Bloomingdale's opening promotion, and we were working on a shoestring budget—struggling just to stay afloat. We paid our employees the best we could, and treated them very well, but we never even considered going union. If we'd had to meet the union's financial demands, we'd never have been able to afford to operate the bakery.

We had no problem with this until a year or so later, when the extent of our business with Bloomingdale's made it necessary for us to move to a larger bakery. Here's where our union problems started. The problem was that Famous Amos had made such a big splash in the media, everybody assumed the company's finances were keeping pace with its celebrity, and the union wanted a piece of the action.

There were two separate attempts to organize the workers at the new bakery. In both cases, it was a very unfriendly, antagonistic process—divisive, destructive, distracting—a real waste of resources because, of course, we had to hire attorneys to fight the attempts—money that would have been much better spent on wages and on growing the business! The employees were divided amongst themselves, and it was just very negative all around. But ultimately, both times, the employees voted against unionizing, and we could get back to business.

My lesson here is that in business, of course you want to control everything, but there are simply certain things about doing business that you have no control over, and yet you still have to deal with them. You can't waste energy moaning about a situation because it's unpleasant. You have to keep focused on your goal and work through the problems that crop up along the way.

Cook's Note: As you work with different recipes, you're bound to find some batters are smoother than others, but there are lessons to be learned in working through the lumps—they may even ultimately enrich the texture. In short, never throw a batter out just because of lumps.

Galettes Brûlées (Burned Cookies)

This recipe is a neat testimony to the indestructibility of The Cookie.
Even though it appeared that a large batch of cookies was ruined,
the outcome was still a very positive one, indeed!

Early on in my first store, at 7181 Sunset Boulevard in Los Angeles, one of the workers burned a batch of cookies. Now, a batch of cookies for a commercial enterprise is a *lot* of cookies. My first reaction was to scream, "Hey, man! You burned my cookies! Do you know how much money you just threw out the window? I mean, there's the ingredients! The use of the equipment! The electricity involved! The time wasted! The labor it took to mix up the dough—that's all gone! You can't recoup those losses! Man, you just *burned all these cookies!!* Aughhhhhhh!"

That was my first reaction. Then I remembered all the times that I'd burned cookies—maybe I'd been thinking about something else, distracted by some other activity, and I'd burned my cookies. Well, I certainly hadn't screamed at myself. So, with that thought, I didn't scream at the employee. Instead, I walked him through the process, explaining what the loss was, what was involved in terms of the time and money that you can never get back. I explained that you can't build a business like that, and I said all of this in a patient, caring, and sensitive way. Well, he got it, and went on to become a better employee as a result.

See, whether or not I had yelled, the cookies would still have been burned. My choice was either to go with my knee-jerk response and vent my anger and frustration; or to keep my eye on the long-term goal, and take it upon myself to educate the person so that (a) I didn't lose that employee and have to start over, training someone new, and (b) instead of having an angry worker who might want to get even with me by burning more cookies on purpose, I strengthened the employee's loyalty and goodwill!

Recipe for This Win-Win Situation

Respond to the problem with a cup of *Forbearance*—do not holler the first hot words that come to mind. Count to ten, if necessary.

Add two tablespoons of *Empathy,* as you imagine how the other person who's made the costly mistake must feel.

Stir in a handful of *Patience,* mixed deftly with *Leadership* as you teach, both by instruction and example.

Complete the recipe with a dash of *Trust* as you give the individual their second chance.

Result: a relationship preserved, increased employee loyalty, less turnover, a lower level of stress in the workplace. And all that got burned was one batch of cookies!

Cooling Time

Hot words are very hard to eat, so Anger is one ingredient that should be purged from your Personal Pantry. There are very few recipes this fiery spice enhances.

How do you handle your anger? Do you control it or does it control you? Do you find yourself yelling at the others who share your kitchen—your wife, children, friends, and coworkers—if they don't do things your way, or jump when you say "jump"?

A friend shared this story with me: One day he took his little boy to a local drive-in for a treat, a sweet kind of father-son adventure. The child ordered a soda, but the extra-large cup didn't quite fit into the car's cup holder. When the car pulled out of the parking lot, the soda spilled. The father got mad at the boy and angrily called him names. The little boy, already upset about spilling the drink, grew frightened and hurt at his father's anger, and began to cry. The man immediately regretted what he'd done and apologized to his son, but it was too late to take back his words. The expedition had been ruined, and what could have been a building block in that relationship was on its way to turning into a very negative memory.

Once angry words leave your mouth, the damage has been done, so think twice before you fly off the handle. Breathe, count to ten, do whatever it takes to modify a knee-jerk reaction. You'll be better off in the long run, and so will those around you.

Cook's Note: Every good baker knows that dishes from the oven need to cool a bit before they can be served. So it goes with angry words. Let them cool before you offer them to others, then see if you can transform them from words that threaten and destroy into words of support and comfort instead—much more nourishing all around!

Cookie Cutting

This recipe is a classic example of different ingredients being called for under different circumstances. It also serves to remind us to do all we can to manage a situation at hand, and trust that if our intentions are honorable, all will work out for the best in the long run.

At one point, there was a great guy working with me at Famous Amos. Treb Heinning was a terrific employee: hardworking, loyal; he would do whatever I asked of him. Treb had been with Disney early on, and part of his training had involved working with balloons. He had an incredible knack for blowing up balloons, so at all our parties, he was the designated Balloon Man.

As much as I liked him, though, he just wasn't a good manager of people and, for whatever reason, had a hard time getting along with others. I moved him around in the business trying to find a position where he'd fit in; but no matter where he was placed, it just didn't seem to work. The problem was that Famous Amos was a people company, and Treb just wasn't a people person at that time. I finally had to ask Sid Ross, the president of the company, to let him go.

Well, Treb was furious, and he made no bones about it. For some time after, he had no kind words about me or Famous Amos. I felt bad about it, but he had to be let go for the good of the company. Treb was an ingredient that just didn't improve the mix. In fact, he actually lowered the quality, so our only course of action was to cut him from the recipe.

Fortunately this story has a happy ending. Treb ultimately got on with his life and formed his own company: Balloon Art by Treb. His early days at Disney were a terrific preparation for his new career, and he has been tremendously successful with his business. The balloon art you see at the Super Bowl, at the Olympics, at the national political conventions and every year at the Times Square New Year's celebration—that's all Treb's! He literally created balloon art, and is now the industry leader.

You see, even though we may not know it, we are always in training for something waiting for us down the road in life. We can never see how what happens to us is going to pay off in the end. I felt bad at the time about letting Treb go, and he certainly felt bad about it. But he was simply the wrong ingredient for the recipe I was creating. Letting him go freed him to move on to achieve the monumental success he's had with his own special recipe. And, by the way, Treb and I have since reconnected and are the best of friends to this day.

Corrective Measures: When experimenting with a new recipe, don't be afraid to try out a variety of ingredients; but if one ingredient repeatedly sours the batter, you have to eliminate it—at least for that recipe. Put it back on the shelf and save it for another dish. In this case, *Stick-to-it-iveness* and *Tenacity* would have been disastrous. *Responsibility, Practicality,* and *Decisiveness* had to prevail.

Pass It On

A truly successful Cook is happiest when everybody at the table shares in the feast. Good fortune is amplified when it is extended to others.

One year at Christmastime, my friend Tracey was looking for a gift for her mother. It was close to Christmas Eve and the store she was in was jammed with last-minute shoppers. To make matters worse, it was lunch hour, so most of the people crowding the store were pressed for time. Tracey noticed with dismay that there were horrendously long lines at every cash register. Nonetheless, she found her gift and then, as luck would have it, discovered a register that had just opened up—no line!

Delighted by her good fortune, she completed her transaction quickly. Then, before she left the store, she walked back to the end of one of the long lines, tapped the last person in line on the shoulder and pointed out the register that had just opened. She told him, "Before you leave this line, share the news with the person in front of you, and tell them to do the same."

Later that afternoon, she was in an office meeting, and a fellow worker told how she'd been waiting in a long line after shopping, when someone had tapped her on the back and . . . Tracey was so excited, she jumped up and said, "I started that!"

It takes so little to set a positive chain reaction like that in motion. Who knows how many lives were touched by Tracey's simple act that day?

Ingredients for This Holiday Trifle

Awareness: Be alive to the situation around you.

Thoughtfulness: What can you do to improve it for others?

Fun: Tracey made a game out of helping others and created something that was fun.

Trial by Fire

This recipe is dear to my heart because it shows how, just like cookies, we are tempered and brought to our full potential through the tests that we face in life. For cookies, it's the time they must spend in the oven. In this particular case, for us it meant literally burning to the ground! But, thank God, the Cookie Never Crumbles, and so it went with Famous Amos.

About a year after we opened, my first store at 7181 Sunset Boulevard was going great guns. We were running a wholesale business out of that location in addition to the retail operation, and we were working 'round the clock! But the bad news was that the workload was placing a terrific strain on that location because it just wasn't set up to handle that kind of volume. We had simply outgrown the location. This made for a very stressful situation.

One day I squeezed into the little cubicle that served as our teensy-tiny headquarters, and I told Sid Ross, the guy who was running the business, "Sid! We've *got* to go find office space!" We also agreed that we needed another bakery to handle the wholesale enterprise. Our plan was to keep the 7181 location for our retail business.

Sure enough, we found a great location for a bakery in Van Nuys, California, on Calvert Street. The Bank of America gave us the loan to enable us to move and set up the location. However, the Van Nuys property wasn't appropriate for the corporate office space we needed, so we kept on looking.

We found our office space in a new commercial development complex in Calabasas, California. It was beautiful—the offices were so nice! We got everything moved, and everyone was so pleased and relieved to have such lovely offices. It was tangible proof of significant growth for Famous Amos. We were movin' up!

Then one day I got a phone call: The whole office complex had burned right down to the ground. All our files, all records of our orders and transactions, our office equipment. Christine Harris, a terrific artist I have the good fortune to be married to, had generously provided a number of her pieces to bless and decorate the offices. All of this work was lost in the fire as well. Everything was gone! We had to regroup, big-time. We moved into temporary offices in Oakwood Apartments, an executive apartment complex. Mark Harris, my brother-in-law, was working with us at the time, and did an absolutely phenomenal job reconstructing records and orders. The way he managed to piece things back together was nothing short of miraculous. We were all playing over our heads at that point—we had to! It was the only way we were going to be able to salvage the situation and stay in business.

At times like these, when suddenly everything's up in the air and it looks as if all bets are off, you have to hang in there. If you do, you will find that others respond to your needs, resources are forthcoming, and the people around you rise to the occasion. And that's just what happened with Famous Amos! It took us months to get back on track, but we did, and The Cookie came back stronger than ever.

Recipe for Recovery

When this kind of disaster strikes, the first ingredient you reach for is *Acceptance*—in large amounts. Never waste energy on anger or resentment. There's a lesson to be learned from whatever's happened, so get right to the business of finding out what it is, and move on to solve the problem.

Next, add *Faith* that the roadblock you're facing may well be a building block to something even better.

Spread *Teamwork* liberally. Working together you can accomplish so much more, and everyone's morale benefits along the way.

Splash with *Perseverance* and *Tenacity*. Don't let yourself get discouraged, and *never* give up!

Networking is a highly beneficial garnish—if you need help, *ask* for it. Put the call out and the universe will respond, but it can't respond if you don't ask!

Cookies on Parade

This recipe always makes me smile—it reminds me of the day I realized a childhood dream, and reinforces the importance of one of my very favorite ingredients: Fun!

The year 1977 was a fantastic one for Famous Amos! We were on the cover of *Time* magazine. Everyone was talking about Famous Amos—we were *the* product! We had just scored a big success bringing cookies into Bloomingdale's. Doing business with Bloomingdale's had necessitated our opening the Nutley bakery, so it was natural for me to look for more business on the East Coast.

Macy's was developing their "Cellar" concept: the trendy kitchen and food boutiques within their stores. It seemed a natural venue for Famous Amos Cookies. I already had a good business relationship going with Macy's in San Francisco, and we'd been so successful at Bloomingdale's that Macy's New York store was very interested in the idea of bringing The Cookie into The Cellar. I met with Ed Finkelstein, the chairman of Macy's, and we set about making it happen.

Whenever I brought Famous Amos into a retail venue, I was like a walking billboard—not only for The Cookie, but for the host store as well. Whenever I did an interview about Famous Amos, I would always mention where the cookies were being sold, so my celebrity status represented a terrific marketing and publicity opportunity for Macy's. And that is how I came to realize one of my childhood dreams!

I was invited to participate in the 1977 Macy's Thanksgiving Day Parade. What a thrill! I can honestly say that it was one of the highlights of my life—I was just so excited to be a part of that great holiday tradition! I mean, as a kid living in New York City, I would go down to see that parade every year. As a parent living in New York, I had taken my children to see the parade. After we moved to L.A., I watched it on TV! What was Thanksgiving without the Macy's Thanksgiving Day Parade?! Millions of people felt that way about this event. Just what was it about this tradition that made it so very special to so many people? Participating in that parade taught me a lesson I've never forgotten.

All the people who were going to be in the parade were told to show up early Thanksgiving morning at the American Museum of Natural History on Central Park West. I arrived at the appointed time to find the place humming with people who'd been working through the night. I found out that all of the parade staff workers are Macy's employees from stores across the country. These people had spent the entire year organizing their part of this huge event, and then Macy's had brought them to New York for the culmination of all their efforts. Macy's had invested in them, and they, in turn, were totally invested in making the parade a success. In addition to that, they all seemed hell-bent and determined to make it as much *fun* as it could possibly be for everyone involved. I'm telling you, the level of excitement and enthusiasm of those folks generated an incredibly powerful synergy. It made a big impression on me.

I had the honor and privilege to participate in three more Macy's Thanksgiving Day Parades—1978, 1979, and 1980, and each year the same joyful commitment abounded. It was impressive to see how creative management on Macy's part was able to inspire and energize their employees year after year.

This observation confirmed my own instincts. See, the whole thing with me and Famous Amos was that it was always fun. Had to be. As a result, I attracted fun things and people into my life and business—fun always found me. I was always able to have fun, and still promote my product to a huge mass audience. Fun and profit can coexist.

Employers take note!

Recipe for a Successful Event

Start with ample amounts of *Vision* and *Imagination* as you plan.

Add *Creativity* and *Competence*.

Toss in a generous cup of *Faith* that all will go well.

Balance *Leadership* with *Appreciation,* so that those who work with you understand your vision, and feel valued.

Sprinkle liberally with *Enthusiasm,* then immerse the entire dish in *Fun*!

 Cook's Note: Walt Disney had Snow White's Seven Dwarves say it years ago: "Whistle while you work!"

When to Mess with a Proven Recipe

In business, just as in recipes, there are certain rules and formulas that are best followed in the pursuit of success. More often than not, you probably want to stick with what has been proven to work. However, sometimes you can justify "messing" with a successful recipe, if your priorities have shifted in terms of the desired result. The following is an example of just such a situation.

I learned one ironclad cookie-business rule the hard way, and that's if you have a choice between opening a store in a great location smack-dab in the middle of a successful shopping center, or opening one just off a main drag, with limited visibility, because the rent is cheaper and the deal is with friends, the smart decision is to go with the location that offers visibility and accessibility. You don't have to be a brain surgeon to see the logic there, but in the case I'm referring to, I made my choice with my heart instead of my head, and the store, an adorable little cookie shop by the way, was a bad investment right from the start. Poor business judgment on my part.

By that time, I knew the recipe for a successful cookie store, but I wanted to do business with my friends, so I shut my eyes to the facts, and the store failed. Experience can be a very tough mentor; the lesson is "Don't mess with a successful recipe!"

But there's another lesson here: There are times when you have to ask yourself, exactly what kind of success are you talking about? Let me give you an example of what I mean.

In 1977 I picked up and moved to Hawaii. Now, this made

absolutely no sense at all from a business point of view. It's a beautiful example of messing with the recipe: Trying to run a business from 2,500 miles away is most definitely not a formula for success! As a matter of fact, it was a horrible business move. I mean, there I was with a two-year-old cookie company that I wasn't managing all that well, even in California! But I had fallen in love with Hawaii back when I'd been stationed here with the U.S. Air Force in 1954, and when I came over in 1977 to sell cookies in McInerny's—a fine old specialty store—I remembered why. After just four days, I told Christine, "We're going to move back here." She told me I was crazy, and maybe I was, but I had always wanted to live here, and it just felt like the time was right.

As I look back, I can certainly see how my moving to Hawaii damaged Famous Amos. The company had been founded on quicksand as it was. By now, the manager of our bakery in Nutley, New Jersey, was constantly butting heads with my manager in California, and I was a fairly ineffectual long-distance referee. The business suffered as a result, and I'm sure that the move played a large role in my ultimately losing the company. But I'll tell you something: While my moving to Hawaii may have been bad for Famous Amos, it was the best thing in the world for Wally Amos! You could say that my decision resulted in The Cookie getting a little beat up, but then, you have to ask yourself, what exactly is The Cookie? It is a business, or is it a life? If I had done what was "best" for the business at the risk of my own personal well-being, Famous Amos would have been even worse off in the long run.

In 1978 I embraced the Unity faith, largely because of my meeting Michael Murphy, the Unity minister here in Hawaii. It has changed my life! I have experienced a profound spiritual rebirth. I have attained a level of peace and connectedness that I doubt would have ever been possible had I stayed in California. Well, who can say what would have happened if I'd stayed in California, but I do know that moving to Hawaii was as critical to my life as starting Famous Amos! What looked like a terrible decision, in terms of a recipe for a successful business, was actually the best decision I could have possibly made, in terms of what it has meant to my life as a successful human being.

Cook's Note: In this cookbook, I am offering recipes for success using a very wide definition of "success." In any recipe for a truly successful life, you need a balance between spirituality, relationships, business, health, and self-esteem. You are the sum total of all the parts of your life—your ingredients. In that respect, you are The Cookie! It's up to you to find the right recipe for you. And, like my decision to move to Hawaii, what might seem like the worst possible ingredient for one aspect of your life might be just exactly what you need to balance out another.

Kiwi Kazoos

One of the things I love about cookies is that there is just nothing formal about them! I have always been amazed at the way a plate of cookies can warm up an exchange. You simply never know when someone you're with would love to let their hair down and have FUN! The following recipe is about exactly that.

I traveled to Australia in 1979 to bring Famous Amos to the folks Down Under. We opened a cookie store in Melbourne, and also sold cookies to Meyers, a fine department store chain throughout Australia. In addition, we got cookies into George's, a very prestigious store in Melbourne. This store was so high-end that the salespeople wore tuxedos! And I sold cookies in this place! I mean, there I was, wearing this mad cowboy hat and a wild outfit, running up and down the aisles of George's, yelling, laughing, playing my kazoo—'cause that's my style. It's just my way of grabbing people's attention, getting them to have fun and to associate having fun with Famous Amos.

By the time I was scheduled to leave Australia, I'd developed some really nice relationships with the folks at George's, from store employees right up to the company board members. The store threw a lovely little farewell reception for me in the boardroom. One of the directors of the company caught my eye. He was a very tall, stately gentleman, the epitome of conservative propriety. I had him pegged for a real sobersides.

Well, true to form, I had taken out my kazoo and was playing goofy tunes and whatnot—having a great time and feeling thankful that I could have such fun in that rarefied atmosphere. Suddenly, this oh-so-proper gentleman exclaimed, "I say, wait a minute!" took a comb wrapped in tissue paper out of his pocket, and joined me on his homemade kazoo!

That was such a neat moment because it showed so clearly how even people who appear not to have an ounce of spontaneity in them are capable of letting their hair down and having fun. The key is for you to have the courage to be who you are in any situation, and not let circumstances or other people's behavior inhibit or diminish you. My playing the kazoo, and just having a wonderful time in that very prestigious setting, gave that formal fellow permission to let himself join in and have fun. It may have been what he'd been wanting to do for ages!

Cook's Note: Clearly the essential ingredients here are *Fun, Spontaneity,* and *Enthusiasm.* Any dish involving these cannot help but be emotionally nutritious to all who partake!

Commitment Miracles

"Letting go and letting God" is what it took to save our marriage. This is a recipe all about saying "I WILL" to God, making a firm commitment, and then stepping back and letting Him take it from there.

At one point my wife, Christine, and I had been having some serious challenges in our relationship: I more than she, for she's been such a supportive, wonderful wife. I was having problems dealing with commitment, and Christine and I were on the brink of going our separate ways. Yet there was a longing deep inside us to acknowledge that we had worked too hard on our marriage, and on our beautiful family, to just throw everything away.

We felt that a marriage-encounter weekend was what we needed to start pulling our marriage back together. And it did so in a very powerful way: The experience brought a spiritual focus to our relationship. During that weekend, we listened as other couples shared their stories, their innermost feelings and emotions. One of the leaders of the marriage-encounter group told us that years ago he had said to his wife, "I love you, and there is nothing you can ever do that would cause me to stop loving you."

That clear statement of commitment really moved me. I was deeply touched by those words because Christine has demonstrated again and again that type of love for me, and I had not always reciprocated. It was time for me to step up and make that kind of commitment to her, and make it in the presence of witnesses.

Right then and there, I took her hands, looked into her eyes and said, "I love you, Christine, and there is nothing you can do that would ever cause me to leave you or stop loving you." I knew that I needed to take an active part in healing our relationship, and that strong, simple statement was what it took to turn my life and my marriage around. As it turned out, it was the first step of our journey back toward each other.

A few weeks later, a friend shed some perspective on that weekend epiphany. He explained that true relationship is not just a commitment to another person. It's saying "I will!" to God. When Christine and I made the commitment to search for a way to save our marriage, we were saying "I will!" to God. That was such a powerful realization! With that awareness, we started in earnest to let go and let God be the focus in our marriage and in our lives. Since then, miracles have happened in our relationship!

Recipe for Commitment Miracles

(For this recipe to succeed, you must acknowledge a Higher Power as the Ultimate Cook in your life.)

Start with a *Relationship* that you believe in.
    Add a large cup of *Commitment*.

Stir in *Faith,* acknowledging the Higher Power that you believe in as the source of everything in your life, including the Relationship.

Add *Focus on Problems and Solutions,* then top with *Trust* that "letting go" will allow whatever needs to happen in the relationship take place.

Reagan Rarebit

*I call this a recipe for "Rarebit" because the experience that pro-
duced it gave me a rare bit of insight into the common spark of
humanity we all share, regardless of rank or station in life.*

During Ronald Reagan's presidency, there was a
Small Business Conference held in Washington, D.C.
It was a series of meetings and sessions, and during
the course of events, I was slated to receive the Small Business
Entrepreneurial Award. In honor of this award, I was invited to a
White House reception where I knew I'd be introduced to Pres-
ident Reagan. This would be the first time I'd ever been to the
White House, to say nothing of meeting the president! I was
very excited by the prospect, to say the least.

Before leaving Hawaii, I spoke to my friend Tom Ruppanner,
who was the president of Aloha United Way—I was on his board
of directors. We had a benefit auction coming up, and I asked
him if there was anything I could bring him back from the
White House. He laughed and said, "Why don't you have President Reagan autograph a $100 bill, and we'll auction it off?"
Well, this was a good idea, all right, but my finances weren't all
that great at the time, so I asked Tom if he could make do with
the president's autograph on a nice crisp $1.00 bill. He allowed
as how he could. I procured two crisp new dollar bills, and
headed off to Washington.

The conference was terrific, and it was very satisfying to be
honored with that award. But it was the White House that
knocked me out. Not just seeing it up close and personal for the

first time, but actually being inside that national monument. The whole building just resonated with history. Then there was the protocol: I mean, marines, the honor guard, the formality of it all!

Following the awards ceremony, we all went upstairs for a little reception—all businessmen, everyone in suits and ties. Everyone, that is, except for me—Wally Amos from Hawaii, in my bright aloha shirt. Wally Amos in a suit just wouldn't be Wally Amos, right?

At the reception, I finally had the opportunity to meet Ronald Reagan. Now everybody knew about the president and his fondness for jelly beans, so I kidded him, "Mr. President, I don't have any jelly beans, but what are your thoughts on chocolate chip cookies?" He laughed, and we had a pleasant little conversation about cookies and jelly beans. I hadn't forgotten the two crisp dollar bills in my wallet! I was waiting for the right moment to ask Ronald Reagan to sign at least one of them.

The opportunity came after the reception, at a photo op in the Indian Treaty Room. Now, at a photo op, everybody lines up, and the president stands at the end of the line, either to the right or the left—in this case, he was off to the right. You wait in the line and move along until it's your turn. There's a Secret Service man at the head of the line to tell you when it's the right time for you to approach the president. On this occasion, Reagan was flanked by a couple of aides.

So, there I was, the lone aloha shirt in the line of suits, inching my way along towards my chance to ask the president of the United States to sign one of my dollar bills. From the speed at which the line was moving, it was pretty clear there was going to be time for only one. I was ready, too, with a pen in one hand, and my crisp new bill in the other. When I was the next in line, the large Secret Service guy looked at me and said, "What are you going to do with that pen?"

I said, "I'm going to ask the president to sign this dollar." He didn't look too happy about that, but before we could have any more conversation, it was my turn, so I just left him standing there, and walked over to Reagan. I figured people knew who I was. I mean, what were they going to do, shoot me?

Well, I went over and had my picture taken with the president of the United States, and then I said, "Excuse me, Mr. President, I'm on the board of directors of the United Way at home. Would you please autograph this dollar? We want to auction it off at our fund-raiser." Reagan smiled and asked one of his aides to turn around so that he could use his back as a surface on which to sign the dollar! I said, "Sir, would you please sign it 'To Aloha United Way.' "

He turned, looked me right in the eye and asked, "You want me to put that on the dollar?" I said, "Yes, sir, please." He nodded, and signed accordingly. Now, here's the gist of the story for me: When he asked me that question, he didn't ask it as the president of the United States—we were absolute equals at that moment. All the barriers, all the titles, all the protocol disappeared. It was simply one human being looking to fulfill the request of another human being.

It was a powerful moment, a real defining moment for me. It drove home the fact that no matter who I'm talking to—title, rank, position notwithstanding—he or she is first and foremost a human being, just like me! That thought helps me to keep my balance, and a proper perspective on the people, places, and events in my life.

Recipe for Re-creating This Equalizing "Rarebit"

Start with a generous serving of *Self-Respect.*

Add one healthy measure each of *Empathy* and *Acceptance* to balance the recipe.

Stir in an ample spoonful of *Trust* that your dish will be received in the spirit with which it's offered.

Be sure not to clutter this recipe with miscellaneous titles and ranks, as these only create lumps and inconsistencies in the texture.

Cook's Note: In the words of a fine old chef, when asked how he handled his butterflies when meeting with high-powered clients: "I just tell myself they put their pants on one leg at a time, just like I do."

Playful Topping

Sometimes things we cherish accomplish even more good in the world after they leave our possession. You just never know!

In honor of the publication of my book, *Watermelon Magic*, my wife Christine painted me a wonderfully whimsical pair of watermelon shoes. My mother-in-law followed suit and gave me a glorious watermelon hat!

I treasured that hat and wore it everywhere I went. It never failed to make people smile, and gave rise to all kinds of interesting exchanges. At one point, I was returning to Hawaii after business on the Mainland, and as I boarded the plane, the pilot admired my special watermelon hat. He warned me that he intended to wrestle me for it. I told him, "Not a chance!"

After we had safely landed in Honolulu, the pilot came out of the cockpit and said he had come for my hat. I told him he couldn't have my hat, no way! Well, he went into a whole song and dance about what a great collection of hats he had, and how my watermelon hat would be the crowning glory of them all. I still said no. Then, all of a sudden, a little voice in my head said, "Awww, Wally, give him the hat."

I took off my prized watermelon hat and presented it to him, on the condition that he would *wear* it, and not just hang it on his wall as a trophy. He agreed, and put it on immediately, beaming from ear to ear.

The next day as I was about to board a plane for another trip, I ran into a friend who was an airline supervisor. He told me he'd just seen the funniest thing—a pilot wearing a watermelon hat in the cockpit, smiling broadly as he backed his jumbo jet out of the gate!

The story doesn't stop there. Sometime later, this particular pilot spotted me as I had dinner between flights in the Dallas airport. He came over to say hello, we chatted, and then I said, "Hey, how come you're not wearing my watermelon hat? I gave you that hat on the condition that you'd wear it, and you're supposed to be wearing it every time I see you—that was the deal!"

Then he told me that a lady who worked in the pilots' office in L.A. was going through some really rough challenges in her life. She had told the pilot that she loved that watermelon hat, and that just seeing the hat brightened her day and made her smile. So he turned around and gave it to her.

I couldn't have asked for a more perfect fate for that hat!

 Cook's Note: Happiness is contagious. Pass it on!

Cookie Break

Even the most passionate culinary artist needs to take a break from their kitchen, so why not go grab yourself some cookies and a frosty glass of milk, and let me tell you a story I really love.

Once upon a time, on a beautiful Saturday morning, two friends set out bright and early for an eagerly anticipated fishing trip. Their plan was to drive to the seashore, meet up with buddies who owned a boat, and sail off for the day.

They hadn't been on the road very long before a tire blew out. Fixing the flat put them about a half hour behind schedule, but they figured their friends would wait, and off they went again. Eager to make up some time, they pushed the pedal to the metal, and sure enough, sailed right by a cop with a radar gun. Bureaucracy being what it is, the ticket cost them fifty bucks and another forty-five minutes.

They had just convinced themselves that as they were bringing the food and drinks for the expedition, their friends would still be waiting for them, when the fan belt snapped.

Two hours, one tow, and an expensive repair later, one said despondently to the other, "I know they wouldn't have waited this long. Let's just cut our losses and go home."

His friend, however, would have none of it. "Nah, I always finish what I start. Let's just go on and see for sure."

He managed to convince his disappointed pal, and they continued on to the agreed-upon meeting place. Sure enough, the pier was deserted, the boat slip empty—their buddies had gone.

The first guy said, "See? I told you. It was just a waste of time coming here. The perfect ending for a loused-up morning."

His friend was on the point of agreeing when they both heard faint voices calling out in the distance. It didn't take long for them to discover a couple of little boys who'd been playing in the surf nearby and gotten sucked out by a strong current. As it happened, our friends were both lifeguards, and were able to reach the boys just in time to save their lives. It was the perfect ending for a loused-up morning.

Isn't that a great story? It certainly doesn't take a brain surgeon to get the point: If everything had gone as those guys hoped, they'd have been long gone when the two little boys needed them. Things happen for a reason. We may not understand at the time just what that reason is, but we have to have faith in the fact that we are all part of a larger Plan. We need to be more accepting of the things that happen in our lives, and trust that they are neither "good" or "bad" in and of themselves, but instead are purposeful experiences that we are constantly moving through on our way to being the very best that we can be.

Remember: The Cookie NEVER crumbles!

6

Pot Luck:

Recipes for Sharing

Karma of the Cookie

*Simply put, the essence of this following recipe is that what goes
around, comes around. In other words, the cookies that you bake
and give away inevitably find their way back to you.*

In addition to my entrepreneurial work, I am a professional public speaker, and spend a great deal of time traveling across the country, giving inspirational/motivational talks to audiences that run the gamut from the employees of Fortune 500 companies, to Unity Church congregations, to schoolchildren in neighborhood libraries. Even as I write this, I am developing "Read Aloud with Wally Amos," a very exciting children's TV project supporting literacy.

How on earth did all of this get started?

Well, in 1979, I was looking for a cause that I could use my celebrity as Famous Amos to support. My friend John Rosica made me aware of the fact that at that time there were approximately 23 million adults in our country unable to read above a fourth-grade level. I was appalled by the number, and could easily see how illiteracy was the root of countless social problems. It was a cause close to my heart, as both my parents were functionally illiterate.

I approached Literacy Volunteers of America and offered them my services. I agreed to become national spokesperson for that organization and began speaking to literacy groups across the country. I was able to use my celebrity to attract attention to the problem and the solutions available. In addition to supporting literacy, I frequently shared my story of how someone like me—born poor and black in Tallahassee, Florida—could go on to create Famous Amos, as a way of encouraging people to achieve their full potential. If I could do it, so could they!

Now, when I started out with LVA, even though I was a celebrity and an experienced promoter, I had no training at all in the art of giving speeches. But I so believed in the cause that I'd just get up in front of whatever group I was addressing and share what was in my heart. It was from doing this over and over with many different groups that I was able to hone my skills as a public speaker.

One thing that helped me tremendously was that as a result of my role as spokesperson for LVA, I got to host five segments in a series of forty-three half-hour shows produced by Kentucky Educational Television called *GED on TV*. This was a series designed to help adults prepare for the General Educational Development exam—the test that would qualify them for a high-school equivalency diploma.

So I hosted five of the reading shows. When that came off well, the folks at Kentucky Educational Television said, "We've got thirty shows that we want to redo," and I hosted all thirty shows in their *Learn to Read* series. Then they said, "We've got fifteen shows called *Another Page,* and we'd like for you to host those," and so I hosted those shows. All told, I wound up hosting fifty half-hour shows. Now, that's a lot of reading! The shows did well, too, and are still running today, because the information they offer is timeless.

That experience gave me skills that made me an even more effective public speaker. It improved my enunciation, my understanding of how to work with words, how to use inflection and emphasis to strengthen the message I wanted to get across to people.

Now, as I work on "Read Aloud with Wally Amos," I'm finding that the skills I developed reading off the teleprompter for the Kentucky Educational Television programs are proving to be absolutely invaluable! Turns out that was the best possible basic training for reading out loud!

So all this started with my offering my services to help out Literacy Volunteers of America. My intention at the time was to give back to the community, but I want to tell you that if I live to be a million years old, I'd still come out the winner! Professional skills, exposure, and fantastic opportunities have all come my way simply because I offered to give myself away to Literacy Volunteers of America, and help adults learn to read.

In a nutshell, then, giving is receiving, in the deepest sense.

Recipe

(This one's very simple: you could even call it a "no-brainer!")

Start with a large bowl of *Giving*—the willingness to give freely of yourself.

Stir in *Commitment* to a cause you believe in.

Add liberal measures of *Energy, Vitality,* and *Enthusiasm.*

Add *Willingness to Learn.*

Leaven with *Cooperation* and *Teamwork.*

Mix all ingredients well, and serve the finished product with a big dollop of *Fun.*

Cook's Note: Volunteering is reaching your hand into the darkness to pull another's hand back into the light, only to discover that it is your own.

Special Friends at My Table

Thanks to my work with literacy, it has been my privilege to spend time in the company of both George and Barbara Bush. I have met George over the course of fairly formal occasions—awards ceremonies, state dinners, official receptions at the White House, and the smaller parties that followed. Barbara and I have worked together more closely, championing the cause of literacy in America.

Whatever you feel about their politics, I believe the Bushes are remarkable people. In addition to their being truly extraordinary individuals, each in their own right, they are also an exceptionally close couple. Their marriage is a strong, loving partnership.

I have great respect for George and Barbara, and cherish the memories I have from my times with them. They've provided several recipes I'd like to share with you. You can bet their Personal Pantries are well-stocked with top-notch ingredients!

Presidential Pastry

In 1990, I received the National Literacy Honors Award from the White House, along with Harold McGraw, a titan in the publishing business and a real community servant, and other adult-literacy students and tutors. The presentations were made by Barbara and George Bush. The reception that followed could easily have been solemn and intimidating but fortunately, this recipe allowed all involved to lighten up and enjoy themselves.

The gala presentation of the 1990 National Literacy Honors Awards was a very prestigious evening affair, with entertainment provided by Barbara Mandrell, Patrick Swayze, and Morgan Freeman. It was a great honor to share the night with such an illustrious group.

This particular event was also the first time their television cameras had ever been allowed inside the East Room of the White House: ABC was recording it to be aired later as a TV special for national broadcast. Gary Smith and Dwight Hemian, two of television's top-quality people, were the producers, and did a beautiful job of it. It was just a wonderful occasion. I received my award, and it was a very somber, very special moment for me.

After the telecast, everyone involved in the ceremony was invited up to the second floor—the living quarters of the White House—for a postceremony party. Well, somehow Christine and I managed to be the first couple to arrive up there. I don't know how it happened, but there we were on our own, so we began looking around. It was just overwhelming—the White House is a living museum! Literally! There's just such a tremendous sense of history to the place. It suddenly struck me then how the power of the office of president is just that—the power of the office: of the title, of all that that building represents. The man who bears the title is honored to possess it only temporarily. His job is to uphold and strengthen it to the best of his ability, and then move on, leaving it for the next incumbent.

I was marveling at that solemn insight as Christine and I continued to admire the history that surrounded us, when at that moment, around the corner came George and Barbara Bush! Well, the very first thing that came to me to do was to whip out my kazoo and play "Hail to the Chief." I think George was a little startled—he didn't seem to know quite what to do—but Barbara started doing a little dance. She has a great knack for adapting to almost any situation.

We all had a nice laugh about it. And you know, it was just another Wally Amos Moment—where Wally Amos believes in having fun, even with the president of the United States! See, if I'd let myself get all intimidated by the office he represented, and squashed my impulse to salute him with my kazoo, we would have all missed out on a really neat memory, and a chance to connect on a very human level.

Recipe for Presidential Pastry

Start with a healthy dose of *Awareness of What's Appropriate*.
Add a strong cupful of *Appreciation* of time and place.

Then leaven the mixture with equal amounts of *Empathy* and *Humor*.

Use a dash of *Good Judgment* to determine how long to work the mix—if underdone, the result will be less than memorable. If overdone, tough and hard to swallow. When this recipe works, it is a delight to all who share a laugh over it.

 Cook's Note: The key here is a very light touch!

"Sole" Food 9

Appreciation *and* Thoughtfulness—*staples in the Relationship Relish group—are the key ingredients in this next recipe.*

My wife, Christine, is an incredibly creative and playful artist. She doesn't limit herself to conventional media. Our house is chockablock with her whimsical work. When I wrote *Watermelon Magic,* she painted watermelons on the toes of a pair of my shoes. I loved the idea so much that I had her "customize" all my shoes! They never fail to make people smile and provoke entertaining remarks. They're a terrific icebreaker in any situation.

Well, one time we had been invited to an official dinner at the White House. The president of South Korea was visiting at the time, and this was a formal state dinner in his honor.

As is always the case with these formal affairs, the entering guests had to pass through a receiving line. I was all dressed up in a tuxedo, but I was still wearing the brightly colored watermelon shoes that Christine had painted for me. We moved down the line until we came to President Bush, who noticed my footgear and said, "Oh, Wally, I like your shoes! They're pretty fancy." I replied, "Well, thank you, Mr. President. My wife Christine, here, painted them, and I'm sure she'd be happy to paint a pair for you also."

George Bush smiled and said, "Wellll, I don't think so, but maybe you could paint a pair for Barbara." We laughed and left it at that, and went on to have a lovely evening.

A couple of weeks passed, and one day back at home in

Hawaii, when I went to the post office to pick up my mail, I found a bulging manila envelope from the president of the United States, addressed by hand to Christine Amos. Well, Christine wasn't around, and my curiosity got the better of me, so I opened it. Inside were several photographs and a personal note from George Bush. The note was asking if Christine would paint a pair of shoes for Barbara, and the photos were of some of the First Lady's favorite things that the president thought she might like represented on the shoes. That just knocked me out! What thoughtfulness, from a man who literally had the cares of the world on his mind at the time!

That was a great lesson to me.

Cook's Note: In the kitchen of your life, no matter how important a dish you're cooking up, keep your priorities in perspective, and never miss an opportunity to show your appreciation for those you love. Even the smallest thoughtful gesture is a very potent spice.

"Sole" Food 11

Spontaneity, Playfulness, and Fun all come into this recipe!

In the course of my work as national spokesperson for Literacy Volunteers of America, I visited Washington, D.C., to do a literacy promotion at the Library of Congress for a group of librarians who would be gathered there that morning. Then we were to go on over to the White House, where Barbara Bush had planned a reception to welcome us.

Now, just prior to this event, Christine had custom-painted a special pair of tennis shoes for Barbara Bush at the personal request of her husband, the president of the United States. We had sent them off to her, and Christine had received a nice thank-you note from Barbara, so I knew she'd actually received them. Anticipating the upcoming schedule of events, I sent Barbara a note saying that I was looking forward to seeing her. I said I would definitely be wearing my specially painted watermelon shoes, (also by Christine, in honor of my book *Watermelon Magic*), and I hoped that she planned to wear hers.

When I gave my little talk at the Library of Congress, I told all of the participants the story of Barbara's painted shoes. I said, "Now, obviously, Barbara's not going to be wearing her painted shoes, but when you guys see her, I want everybody to ask her, 'Barbara, where are your painted shoes?' Let's see if we can talk her into putting on her painted shoes."

When we got over to the White House for the reception, and everyone was seated in the East Room, Barbara sent for me to say hello. I went back to visit with her in the anteroom where she was waiting. She just looked great, as always—beautifully put together, with her mane of white hair, red-and-white polka-dot dress with the little pearls, and a nice pair of neutral-colored pumps.

We were standing there talking, and all of a sudden she looked down and saw my shoes. Eyes twinkling, she said, "Wally, I bet you want me to put on my painted shoes, don't you?"

I said, "Barbara, come on! You're the First Lady of the land! You—wear painted shoes in the White House???! I wouldn't dream of asking you to do such a thing!"

She looked around and asked, "Are there any members of the press here today?" There weren't, so Barbara asked her assistant to go up to her closet and bring down the painted shoes. And there—in the anteroom of the East Room of the White House—Barbara Bush put them on! We sat together on a sofa, and someone took a photograph which I treasure to this day.

When we finished taking pictures there, we hugged and said our alohas, and I went back out to my seat in the rear of the room. A few minutes later, Barbara entered. When she'd gotten about three-quarters of the way down the aisle, I yelled out from the back of the room, *"Look at those shoes!"* And everybody in the place cracked up—Barbara Bush included!

It was a nice moment. Again, it was a "Wally" moment. I mean, I did what I did because it felt right to me to do it—even though she was the First Lady, and we were in the middle of a White House reception. I was just being myself, and Wally Amos is the same wherever he is! I know it's a fine line to walk, but it's almost always a better choice to have the courage to be who you are under any circumstances, than to be plugged up and intimidated by protocol.

Cook's Note: Although style and presentation are important to a dish, they should never overshadow the contents of the dish itself.

7

Creative Menu Balancing:

Recipes from Losing Famous Amos and Still Going Forward

Resilience Roll-Ups:

OR, THE COOKIE BY ANY OTHER NAME
WILL TASTE AS SWEET

This is one of the most complicated recipes I ever created!

When The Famous Amos Cookie Company found itself in serious financial straits, I tried to remedy our situation by taking in other investors. As a result, I started down the path that would eventually result in my losing control of the company. My role in the company was downsized again and again as it continued to change hands over the next three years. Early on in this slide, I had to renegotiate my contract with the company, and part of the new contract was a noncompete agreement that barred me, for a period of twenty-four months after the termination of my contract—for whatever reason—from conducting business on behalf of any other organization engaged in the production or marketing of cookies.

By 1989, the owners had made it clear that they wanted me completely out of the picture. It was obvious to me then that I'd come to the end of the road as Famous Amos. Talk about having to let go! It was so hard to walk away from a business that had defined my identity and shaped my life for fourteen years!

I used the time well and turned my attention to working and speaking for various charities. I increased my commitment to Literacy Volunteers of America and my support of Communities in Schools. I joined the board of directors of Aloha United Way in Hawaii, and became a member of the board of trustees for the Napoleon Hill Foundation, created by Napoleon Hill, author of *Think and Grow Rich.* This organization teaches people to build self-esteem by adhering to seventeen basic principles, the most important of which is PMA—Positive Mental Attitude. It was a natural cause for me to support, as I demonstrate their principles every day of my life! Since I had to support my family, I also began to pursue a professional speaking career.

These activities certainly kept me busy and fulfilled, but in 1991, I began to get the itch to make and sell cookies again. I had been away from Famous Amos for two years by then, and my noncompete agreement with the company was no longer in force. I decided to start Chip & Cookie—a business built around two adorable chocolate chip cookie character dolls that Christine had created. I planned to call the business "Wally Amos Presents Chip & Cookie," in order to take full advantage of my name and reputation in promoting the venture. Well, the people at Famous Amos had a very different interpretation of the agreement, and they sued me, saying that they owned the rights to "Wally Amos," not only for food products, but for everything—*and* they said they owned it in perpetuity!

This lawsuit was devastating to the Chip & Cookie enterprise, which had really been gathering steam. By then we had Chip & Cookie boutiques in all five J. C. Penney stores in Hawaii. We had a book. We had dolls. We had a line of ceramics, T-shirts, aloha shirts, and three kinds of cookies! I'd been traveling to promote the book. In fact, it was the publicity that I had generated that caught the attention of the Famous Amos people and became the basis of the lawsuit. Because of the lawsuit, we had no choice but to fold the Chip & Cookie enterprise. This was financially devastating, as I'd poured money into start-up expenses, and now had no way to recoup my investment. And I was facing the enormous expenses of a legal battle!

But I didn't roll over, I bounced back—and that's the most important point of this story. As serious as it was, I didn't focus on the lawsuit, I got an attorney to handle that. Chip & Cookie had given me the taste of being back in business, so now my goal was to sell cookies again, and that's where I put my energy and commitment. I couldn't use the name "Wally Amos," but I went ahead and started my new company, and the name I settled on came right out of the circumstances—Uncle Noname. You see, I chose to focus on answers and solutions instead of dwelling on the negativity of the lawsuit. The crisis of losing my name actually became a springboard for creativity.

The long and short of it is that despite the lawsuit, I went forward with my business. Seven months into the battle, I started the new company and began selling Uncle Noname cookies here in Hawaii. I refused to let the circumstances stop me—the only thing that could have stopped me was my giving up. The lesson is that we must learn how to get on top of circumstances instead of living under them! Thirteen months into the lawsuit, I published my book, *Man With No Name*, all about how when life gives you lemons, you make lemonade—something I was going through at the time!

Nineteen months into the lawsuit, the Famous Amos Company gave up and settled out of court in what was a win-win arrangement—actually, the arrangement I'd proposed at the outset of the lawsuit. They retained rights to "Wally Amos" for any business involving food; I regained the rights to my name for any nonfood endeavor. I also got back the rights of publicity, which meant I could use my name, likeness, and reputation to market and promote any product, as long as I didn't call the company Famous Amos or "Wally Amos." Well, this was certainly a win for me, after a long, hard fight. Plus, they paid me $50,000!

Funny how life works—I mean, *they* sued *me*. And then they turned around and paid me to be able to settle out of court because they were looking to sell the company and needed to get rid of the lawsuit before they could close the deal. I'll say it again—you just have to stay in the game! If you hang in there long enough, you're bound to win!

Recipe for Resilience Roll-Ups

Start with large amounts each of *Faith* and *Focus*. I never lost faith that the lawsuit would be settled in my favor, and focusing on my goal of developing Uncle Noname kept me from sinking into the negativity of the lawsuit.

Add *Acceptance*—do not waste energy fighting a problem. Once you separate your emotions from the facts you can gain control of the situation and take the necessary steps to resolve it.

Stir in *Commitment* and *Tenacity*. Without an *"I WILL SUC-CEED"* attitude, this would have been a surefire recipe for failure.

Sprinkle liberally with *Enthusiasm*. *Enthusiasm* creates joy and joy attracts energy. Positive energy attracts the support critical to the success of this recipe.

Toss in *Generosity*—the energy you generate by giving of yourself, even in the lowest times will greatly enrich your recipe.

Moisten continuously with *Responsibility, Honesty,* and *Integrity*. These three ingredients are vital to the essence of the dish. If you stint on any of them, the outcome will be hopelessly compromised.

Cook's Note: George Bernard Shaw said, "I don't believe in circumstances. The people who get on in the world, are those that get up and look for the circumstances that they want."

In other words, never let your kitchen limit or define you. Determine what it is you need for a recipe, then go out and get it.

Group Goodies:

OR, LETTING THE SOUS-CHEFS HAVE THEIR SAY

Interesting that even having been a "sous-chef" in a number of "kitchens" myself, once I became a "chef," I still had a lot to learn!

Seven months into the nineteen-month-long lawsuit over the use of my name, I got the itch to get back into the cookie business, and launched the Uncle Noname cookie company in 1992. I really threw myself into the enterprise, and yet, by 1995, we had made little progress in the market, despite the tremendous effort I was putting out. I felt really bad. I knew I was one-sixth of the team I had assembled, and yet I assumed that since I was the "famous" founder, responsibility for the success or failure of the company rested squarely on my shoulders. I was traveling 75 percent of the year for Uncle Noname, and yet it seemed for every two steps forward, we took four back. Resentment was building up inside me, and I was beginning to wallow in "Poor Me" energy.

At a meeting we held in October 1995, I started complaining about how much I was traveling, how hard I was working, and how little we seemed to have to show for it. One of my associates simply said, "Well, Wally, maybe you shouldn't travel so much." That succinct statement pulled me up short.

The truth was that no one but me was asking me to work harder than everybody else, nor was it necessary! My turning myself into a victim only blinded me to the potential contributions of my partners. By insisting on trying to do it all, I was actually stonewalling what they might have to offer. I had forgotten that it was the Uncle Noname Company, not the Wally Amos Show. I vowed then and there to step back into line and work as a member of the team.

Positive results were immediately forthcoming. Once I was willing to listen, my associates were able to convince me that the cookie category was too crowded, and that we didn't have the resources to succeed with yet another brand. Lou Avignone suggested that we needed a "niche" product—something in a less-crowded category. With Lou at the helm, our team decided to launch a line of fat-free gourmet muffins. They put a program together without any help from me, and Uncle Noname was on its way.

In 1999, when I rejoined Famous Amos as spokesperson, Uncle Noname evolved into Uncle Wally's Muffins, and we are now the only company to offer fat-free gourmet muffins in stores nationally! We've grown to a successful, full-line muffin company, offering multiple varieties of sugar-free and full-fat muffins in addition to the original fat-free versions.

While I was building Famous Amos, I never imagined I'd eventually be involved in selling anything but cookies. But when the time came to cross over, I had to be able to let go of my own ego and listen to Lou Avignone's counsel. I'm so glad I did! Relationships and connections have come about as a result of Uncle Wally's Muffin Company, that even as I write are helping to start up another new enterprise!

Recipe for Creative Collaboration

Before undertaking this approach to any recipe, review the underlying principle of *Teamwork*:

*T*ogether *E*veryone *A*chieves *M*ore

With this concept fully understood and accepted by all participants, regardless of the dish you are going to create, reach for the following ingredients:

Humility: Accept the fact that no one member of the team is more important than another.

Appreciation: Enjoy the different strengths each member brings.

Flexibility: Be able to assimilate different approaches.

Clarity: Keep everyone on the same page.

Respect: Listen closely, and honor other's ideas with attention.

Patience: It takes time to hear other points of view, instead of simply insisting on being "right."

Enthusiasm: Keep the team energy up and moving forward.

FUN: The reason for this ingredient is self-evident!

Back-Burner Beauties:

It is an honor and a privilege to have a very gifted artist as a wife. This next recipe was inspired by her brainchildren!

Christine first came up with the idea for Chip & Cookie back in 1987. She created two adorable little chocolate chip cookie plush dolls—a boy and a girl— and I just fell in love with them. We had some friends who had access to doll manufacturers in the Philippines who arranged for the original prototypes to be created. We were moving right along until they were faced with major distractions with their business, and the project got derailed for the time being.

Then, in 1991, after I had left Famous Amos, I picked it up again. I had passed through my period of mourning over the loss of the company, and was itching to start up another business. I introduced Chip & Cookie to J. C. Penney's in Hawaii. Penney's created Chip & Cookie boutiques in all five of their stores. By this time, in addition to the dolls, we had developed a whole line of Chip & Cookie products: We had cookies, dolls, T-shirts, aloha-wear; our friend Kay Miura designed a line of ceramic teapots, teacups, and cookie jars all featuring Chip & Cookie. We were really moving forward until the lawsuit over the use of my name knocked us off track again and resulted in the collapse of the company.

But Chip & Cookie was a concept that I loved. It was such a strong concept that I just knew it was going to work—all I had to do was to figure out *how.* I kept looking for the opportunity to get it back up and going again. We had another false start with the Gund Toy Company, known for high-quality dolls. Bruce Raiffe, the president and owner, a friend of mine, was interested, but ultimately this shot misfired because their concept for the product just didn't line up with mine.

Time passed, and then came the ascent of the Internet as a marketplace. I saw all sorts of possibilities open up and got excited about Chip & Cookie all over again! I said to myself, "I bet I could set up a Web site, and market Chip & Cookie that way."

I called Leslie Harrington, the professional designer who'd worked with Christine's original idea and had produced a commercial version of Chip & Cookie. I asked her to redesign and update the dolls. I went about setting up a Web page.

Then, in May 2000, I attended a conference with Sam's Club in Arizona. As you know, Wal-Mart owns Sam's Club. Now, I do a lot of business with both Wal-Mart and Sam's Club, as a result of Uncle Wally's Muffin Company, and I've developed great relationships with the top executives in both of those companies. At that conference, Lee Scott, the president and CEO of Wal-Mart said something that kind of stuck with me. He said, "We want our suppliers to be biased toward Wal-Mart and Sam's. If you have a new idea, *we* want to see it first!"

That started me thinking. I looked at the new Chip & Cookie designs, and I thought about that statement. Wal-Mart has 3,500 stores! If I could get Chip & Cookie products into Wal-Mart—well, you do the math! It could really be exciting. So I sent a letter off to Lee Scott and reminded him of his statement, saying I did have a new idea, and was very biased toward Wal-Mart. I asked him to arrange for me to meet with the appropriate people at Wal-Mart.

While all this was happening, I had sent the dolls to a friend of mine, Wayne Easterling, who is the president of DMA, a big premium promotional company in Dallas, just to see what he thought. He went ahead and made up samples for me—at no charge! Then he contacted an apparel designer that his company worked with, and she started designing a line of Chip apparel for boys and a Cookie line for girls! Then he introduced me to a puzzle guy, and then to a specialty houseware designer, as well as a manufacturer that produces backpacks! Suddenly I had all of this Chip & Cookie product!

Then came the opportunity to tie in with Golden Books—the largest supplier of children's books to Wal-Mart! I had been e-mailing Chip & Cookie material to Rich Collins at Golden Books, and when I was in New York on business in September, I called him to see if we could have a meeting as I was passing through. Not only did he say yes, but it turned out that Doug Covington, the representative who serviced the Wal-Mart account for Golden Books happened to be in town that day, so Rich brought him into the meeting.

This was the final piece of the puzzle! See, the mission behind Chip & Cookie is to promote reading, but the one product element that had been missing was a book! Random House had said no. Scholastic had said no. But Golden Books said, "Yes, we want to be a part of this!" Thus the literacy element fell into place!

And all this happened in only five months! To cut to the chase: On November 7, 2000, the team of people who had been collaborating on different aspects of the Chip & Cookie concept joined me in a meeting with the top executives at Wal-Mart to present the product line. It had been a thrilling journey—a creative process galvanized by the deadline of the meeting; and as terrific as that meeting turned out to be, it was not an end in itself. We all regarded it as the door that would open the way to further opportunity, which it most certainly did.

There's such a great lesson here! You can have the most wonderful idea in the world, but if it is not time for that idea to happen, then there's nothing you can do to make it come to pass. You can push it, pull it, put your shoulder to it; but strain and struggle as you might, if the time is not right, your efforts will be in vain.

However, when the time is right, just try and stop it! Chip & Cookie is a perfect case in point!

1987: Great idea, not time for it yet, and the primary facilitators drop out.

1991: Great idea, gets a bit further, but along comes the lawsuit—with necessary lessons for me to learn, at the expense of Chip & Cookie.

May 2000: *Time is ripe!* Wal-Mart & Sam's Club executive interest leads to promotional connection in Dallas, leads to apparel designer, leads to puzzle, backpack, and melamite connections, and bingo!—we have a strong line of Chip & Cookie products! Meanwhile, serendipitous connection loops Golden Books and literacy back to Wal-Mart! But none of this remarkable synergy could have happened before this point in time.

It's the networking and connections I've formed since our initial Chip & Cookie launch in 1987 that have really greased the way for this potentially tremendous success! Back in 1987, I never dreamed this idea could fly so high!

I should also point out that ideas have you, you do not have them. The idea to bring Chip & Cookie to the marketplace took on a life energy of its own, and simply would not turn me loose. It forced me to follow through.

Recipe for Back-Burner Beauties

Start with equal measures of *Creativity, Imagination,* and *Originality.*

Stir in *Enthusiasm* and *Energy.*

Add *Faith* in the ultimate success of the recipe.

Heat up the ingredients with *Initiative,* but should the mixture not blend as expected, remove from the fire and add a cup each of *Acceptance* and *Patience.*

Use a tablespoon each of *Judgment* and *Intuition* in timing when to move the pan back onto the heat.

A large measure of *Stick-to-it-iveness* is essential at all stages of preparation.

This recipe may take several passes to and from the stove, and benefits immeasurably from sprinkles of *Relationships* and *Networking.*

Garnish with *Serendipity* for a really spectacular treat.

8

Specialties of the House:

Recipes for Domestic Success

"Nothin's as Lovin' . . . !"

There's no question that giving is receiving, and nowhere is that clearer than when sharing something you have created yourself.

There's a wonderful energy involved in giving cookies away to people. It's what got me hooked in the first place! It was the satisfaction that people got from something as uncomplicated as a handful of cookies that really turned me on. People always responded so strongly to the fact that I'd invested time, energy, and materials in creating something for them, when in fact, all I had done was to share the result of something I enjoyed doing anyway!

There's a great parallel with relationships here: When you give someone cookies, you give them nutrition that they can take into their bodies, absorb into their systems, and transform into energy and strength. In a relationship, your heart is your oven, and your love is the cookies you offer. When you give someone your love, you're giving them emotional and spiritual cookies! Just as in relationships, though, you always want to be careful to give someone what they want, not what you want them to have.

To further the cookie analogy: If you know someone really craves your chocolate chip cookies, and you insist on giving them pecan chip cookies, because that's what you want them to have, for whatever reason, the gift is diminished significantly. In that instance, offering the cookies—whatever form the "cookies" take—becomes about being in control, not about offering a gift.

Cook's Note: Make sure that when you offer your cookies, there are no dangling strings.

Teamwork in the Kitchen:

INGREDIENTS FOR A SUCCESSFUL MARRIAGE

I've been married three times and have had a number of relationships during the course of my life—some good, some not so good. Now you could either say, "So who's he to give advice on successful marriages?!" Or you could say, "I guess he's been-there-done-that. He must know what he's talking about." If I were you, I'd pick the latter.

Perhaps one of the biggest challenges in maintaining a relationship is that we start thinking of it as just that—taking care of The Relationship. The institution becomes the priority, instead of the other way around! When you get involved with someone, it's the connection between the two of you that makes the magic. Then the tendency is to start codifying things, and the special chemistry gets formalized and defined as Our Relationship or, if it goes far enough, Our Marriage. When the bumps and rocky patches inevitably crop up, the first response is How to Save the Marriage, instead of looking for the chemistry and friendship that started the ball rolling in the first place!

Think about it. You're friends before you assume the roles of Husband or Wife, right? As you grow along with someone, you have to keep that in mind. As friends, you want to keep appreciating each other as individuals, not as objects to be owned—*My* Wife, *My* Husband. As such, you can get trapped in static roles and begin taking each other for granted, which leads to closing off and withdrawing—death knells to any kind of partnership.

I find the idea of the "Tao of Togetherness" really appealing. For me, this is what it means: be fully present for each other; nourish the energy and chemistry that is between you; stay in touch with the friendship that connected you in the first place; and, most importantly, give the people you love what *they* want, not what *you* want them to have.

Cook's Note: You want a special place in your Personal Pantry for your relationship ingredients, and make sure the following are always topped up:

Unconditional Love, Passion, Friendship, Acceptance, Commitment, Responsibility, Honesty, Integrity, Patience, Forbearance, Understanding, Generosity, Respect, Faith, Trust, Fun, Curiosity, Appreciation, Empathy, and *Perspective.*

The Truth About Eggs: Practical Yolks

One of the hardest things in life is letting go. To let something go means you have to break off a relationship, whether it's with a situation, a possession, or a person. It's always hard to separate yourself from something in your life that was once very important to you. It's something we all have problems with at one time or another.

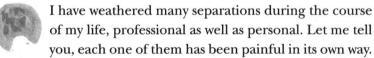 I have weathered many separations during the course of my life, professional as well as personal. Let me tell you, each one of them has been painful in its own way. But the good news is that each separation had to happen in order for me to be able to move forward with my life and business. I never would have achieved what I have with Famous Amos had I not left my first job in the supply room at Saks, or my position as agent with the William Morris Agency, or my career as a freelance talent manager in Los Angeles; and yet each of those professional situations have added knowledge and experience that are invaluable to me today.

I have lived through two divorces, neither of which was easy, but had I not moved on from Maria and Shirlee, I never would have learned the lessons that have made the wonderful marriage Christine and I share possible. I wouldn't even have been available for this relationship!

During the course of my building Famous Amos, there were times I had to release employees and managers in order to keep the company moving in a positive direction—I even had to let my ex-wife Shirlee go when she just wasn't working out as cashier at my Sunset Boulevard store. None of it was easy, but it had to be done.

So what's "The Truth About Eggs"? Simply this: You can't create dough without breaking some eggs! You just have to be mindful of the irrevocability of the act, and think things through as much as possible. Once an egg is broken, circumstances are set in motion that cannot be reversed.

Another thing to remember is that when an egg is broken, there are many ways it can be used that may not have been part of your original intention. Eggs I have broken in my life have surprised me over and over again by reappearing in other excellent recipes!

 Cook's Note: Pull these ingredients off the shelf when you know you'll be working with eggs:

Focus: Be clear about what you want to accomplish, and whether the circumstances surrounding you are actively helping you toward that goal.

Decisiveness: When it feels like you've got to move on, you've got to move on. Do it and don't look back.

Self-Confidence: Trust your instincts.

Faith: Know that when you break an egg to make dough, what may appear to be a destructive act is really part of the creative process.

The Truth About Ovens, 4

This recipe goes back to one of my original statements: while you may not be able to understand the purpose behind what feels like a painful experience at the time, you simply have to trust that there is a Larger Plan at work, and look for the lesson you are being asked to learn.

A while back, my wife, Christine, our daughter Sarah and I went on a family vacation that included six days in Paris. We were delighted that my middle son, Gregory could fly up from Barcelona, where he's currently living and working, to spend some time with us in the City of Light.

On our second day together, we decided we'd be tourists, even though it was raining like crazy. Each of us had something we particularly wanted to see. We visited the Eiffel Tower, grateful that the rain had discouraged the crowds. We stopped to see Napoleon's tomb. Gregory's choice was the Rodin Museum, so after lunch, that's where we headed.

There are two parts to that lovely museum—the interior of the building, and the outdoor sculpture garden. We chose to see the garden first. We were looking around, awed by the splendor of Rodin's work, when Gregory wandered off on his own. Right about the time I noticed he'd gone on, I heard a bloodcurdling scream from another part of the garden. I knew at once it was Gregory. He wasn't far away; we were separated only by a hedge. I raced around the corner of it to find him lying on the ground. The morning's heavy rains had left big puddles all over the garden. Gregory had tried to jump over one of them, lost his footing on the slippery flagstones, and come down hard, fracturing his right kneecap. He was writhing in agony.

The French emergency service couldn't have been more efficient. An ambulance was quickly called to the scene and whisked Gregory to a hospital near Notre Dame Cathedral, where he was given morphine for the horrendous pain, X-rayed, and stabilized. By the way, never once did anyone ask me for our insurance status, or how we planned to pay for all of this care! Despite the language barrier, I eventually worked it out with the business office that I would send a check to cover the costs, but it was clear when we came in, the hospital's priority was taking care of my son, not figuring out the bill.

The upshot was that Gregory was going to have to stay in the hospital for seven days while Christine, Sarah, and I continued on to Amsterdam. After we got him settled in his room, he asked me to get in touch with Maribel, his girlfriend in Barcelona, to see if she would come be with him during his recuperation, and then help him make the trip back to Barcelona. Actually, this meant calling a friend of Maribel's who spoke English, and would be able to translate what had happened to Gregory. Maribel was there that next morning.

Now, before Gregory had joined us in Paris, he'd only just gotten back together with Maribel for about a week. The relationship had had its difficulties, and at this point, was pretty tenuous. Nevertheless, she dropped whatever she was doing to come and be with him. He and I had a little talk about this. I said, "You know, Gregory, this really says a lot about the integrity of this woman and her feelings for you. Whatever fears you're having, whatever reluctance to making a commitment, you need to take another look at the relationship."

The bottom line is that Gregory's accident in the Rodin

Museum sculpture garden really brought the two of them closer together, and strengthened their relationship immeasurably. Maribel was still there later that week when Sarah, Christine and I left, and she stayed by his side until he was released from the hospital. They went back to Barcelona together, and seem well on their way to forging a strong life-partnership.

This is just such a beautiful example of how you can never know why something happens, or what good may come out of a painful situation. It seems to me that this was a wake-up call to Gregory, a time-out for him to stop and look into his heart. Whatever the reason, he'd resisted making a serious commitment to this wonderful woman who clearly loved him. It's as if he had to break his knee in order to stop running away. Once he stopped running, he could appreciate what they had together, and choose to commit to it.

 Cook's Note: See the next story.

The Truth About Ovens, 44

This is actually a little aside, just to piggyback that last story about Gregory and Maribel, but the conversation I had with Gregory in that Paris hospital brought to mind my own epiphany with Christine.

Christine and I started seeing each other in New York City in 1976 and moved to Hawaii together in 1977. We weren't married at the time—hadn't even discussed that possibility—but we were close, and living together very comfortably.

Well, in 1978 or 1979, I met a lady in New York City, started seeing her, and Christine and I separated. The separation lasted seven or eight months. Then I came to the realization that while this other lady was a lovely person, she wasn't the one I wanted to spend my life with. Christine was that person, and for some reason, I had run away from her.

In order to work through this discovery, I had to face the fact that all my life I had run from serious emotional commitments; that whenever I got too close to being locked into a relationship, I always found a way out. In fact, I would never go into a relationship without leaving the back door open, so that if I didn't like the way it was going, I always had an exit strategy! Much like a venture capitalist.

When it finally occurred to me that Christine really did love me, I had to ask myself, during the course of a lifetime, how many people do you have the good fortune to come across— other than your mother—who really love you? I needed to look long and hard at that—and I did. And when I stopped and focused on it, I knew that I truly loved her, too. We reconciled, I asked her to marry me, and we have had twenty-five phenomenal years together. I'm not saying they've all been easy—marriage is full of ups and downs, but then so is life. The point is that to have a truly committed relationship, you have to commit. Period. Stop running and close that back door.

Cook's Note: (This holds true for both stories.) Focused heat is critical to the baking process. If you want to make a batch of quality cookies, you have to keep the oven door closed! If you leave the door cracked even a little bit, the heat is diffused, and the cookies compromised.

9

Divine Desserts:

God in Your Kitchen

Notes from a "Super" Chef

A quadriplegic himself, as a result of a tragic horseback-riding accident in 1995, onetime "Superman" Christopher Reeve is committed to spreading awareness about the struggles people with disabilities cope with on a daily basis. His courage as a champion for the disabled is an inspiration to all.

Not long ago, Christopher Reeve was chosen to receive the Heroes Award from Heart of America, a national organization that facilitates involvement of youth in community service. He was invited to attend the ceremony and accept the award in person. There was no honorarium accompanying this award, so he did not benefit financially by actually being there. Although paralyzed from the neck down, and completely dependent on complicated technical life-support paraphernalia, he agreed to make the round trip from his home in New York City to Washington, D.C., out of his unselfish desire to support Heart of America.

This was no ordinary gesture; just look at what was involved in his journey! It took three hours to prepare the plane because of the extra equipment needed to sustain his life. Loading him into it was a precarious operation because the slightest jar could be fatal. Upon landing, the same care needed to be taken to transfer him from the plane to a specially equipped van. The van transported him to where the awards ceremony would take place; then more complicated maneuvering to get him into the building, and allow him a rest backstage. Quite an operation, wouldn't you say? And all that had to happen before he accepted the award and delivered his speech!

I had the privilege of introducing him. I gave him my biggest kazoo fanfare. He came onstage unattended in his wheelchair, spoke for maybe twenty minutes, and was gracious enough to allow photo-op time. He chatted with people backstage for perhaps another twenty minutes, and then began the laborious return trip. Eight hours of effort for a relatively short appearance!

Anyone would agree that trip was a daunting undertaking, but Christopher Reeve was absolutely committed to setting an example for the youth of our nation. He was willing to give freely of his time and precious energy to support them and demonstrate what true courage and strength really are.

During Christopher Reeve's appearance, someone remarked that he had gone from playing Superman to *being* Superman. How can we who have strong healthy bodies do less?

Cook's Note: Christopher Reeve is an example of an individual who showed his true colors and really rose to the challenge when faced with the calamity that struck his life. I'm sure if you asked him the ingredients he keeps in his Personal Pantry they would include:

Acceptance, Courage, Stick-to-it-iveness, Faith, Giving, Leadership, Patience, and *Forbearance.*

Those are fine ingredients for a Super-Hero Sandwich!

Acknowledge the Ultimate Cook

It's so important to keep a healthy perspective as you define yourself in relationship to the world around you. This cooking tip is all about balance in terms of identity and orientation.

You know, when I started Famous Amos, in my own mind I was The Cookie. I would even tell people, "*I am* The Cookie!" And then look what happened: I lost The Cookie! Talk about cause for a crisis! I mean, if *I am* The Cookie, then what does it mean when *I lose* The Cookie?! I watched The Cookie slip away, and there went my identity! Who was I going to be if The Cookie was gone? Things looked pretty bleak at that point. But remember that song by Sam the Sham and the Pharaohs I told you about earlier (Chocolate Chip Cookie Rock 'n' Roll), "That's Good/No, That's Bad"? Well, I have to tell you that losing The Cookie was just about the best thing that could have happened to me!

I found out that I wasn't The Cookie; I wasn't a business; I wasn't Famous Amos. I had to come to terms with the fact that what I am is a child of God—spirit! Who I am—my essence—is invisible to the human eye and intangible to the human touch. From there I was able to accept that God is the source of everything in my life. My ideas don't come from me, they don't start with me, they come from God through me—I am just the agent for His work. I found such peace in that acceptance! Encouragement, too, because if I accepted the fact that my idea for Famous Amos and The Cookie had come from God, (and I was pretty certain God wasn't a one-idea God), then I could have faith that surely he'd have at least one more idea for me to carry out! That thought was what really pulled me through my darkest times, and God has since given me so many wonderful ideas that it's all I can do to keep up with Him!

The fact that God will not let you fail has been proven over and over in my life: when my parents divorced, Aunt Della and chocolate chip cookies came into my life; when my ultimatum to Saks Fifth Avenue backfired, along came the opportunity with the William Morris Agency; just when my show-business career was foundering, God gave me the idea for Famous Amos, and the faith to go forward with that enterprise. When I was losing Famous Amos, it was because He had a very important spiritual lesson to teach me, so that even though it looked like I was losing, I was gaining! When I look back, it is just so clear to me: Life is never really what it seems, it's always *more!* It's *always* like that, and if you don't believe me, review your own life!

Cook's Note: As you work in the kitchen of your life, always remember that God is the Ultimate Cook. You may be the agent for the dishes you create, but He is the source for the recipes, and the ingredients; He dictates how and when the mixing shall occur; He determines the outcome of each dish. If you accept this reality, there is no limit to what you will be able to achieve.

In the Eyes of the Ultimate Cook, a Cookie Is a Cookie Is a Cookie

Being born black in Tallahassee, Florida, in 1936 meant that I started out with a serious strike against me. Segregation was accepted as the rule of the day, held firmly in place by Jim Crow laws. The world I grew up in accepted as a given the superiority of white people, and the message to me as a black child was: You are a second-class citizen. Accept it; deal with it; don't reach above yourself.

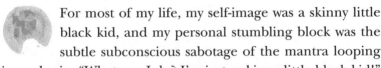 For most of my life, my self-image was a skinny little black kid, and my personal stumbling block was the subtle subconscious sabotage of the mantra looping in my brain: "What can I do? I'm just a skinny little black kid!" In fact, my turning point in terms of freeing myself of that image didn't come until 1997 when I was sixty-one years old! I was in El Paso, Texas, visiting my friend Romeo DiBenedetto and his wife, Victoria. They are both highly spiritual people: he a former Catholic priest and she an ex-nun. Romeo helped me to understand how God's light is manifested in every single one of us, and that thanks to His light shining through me, I am also the Light. Throughout my visit, with Romeo's help, that's what I meditated on: "I am the Light!" That enlightenment set me free and absolutely transformed how I thought about myself.

When I talk to black kids in schools and communities and address the issue of prejudice and the negatives they still have to deal with in our society, I tell them my story. Then I stop and say, "Oh, and by the way, I'm black. I don't know if you realize this or not, but when I started Famous Amos, I was black, and I have it on good authority that I'm gonna be black for the rest of my life. Black is simply the color of my skin!"

The point is that the color of your skin does not affect your mind, your talent, your imagination—unless you let it! There is no such thing as a "black brain," or a "black mind." It's your mind and your brain that create your reality. If you say, "I can't do something because I'm black," or ". . . because I'm female," or ". . . because I'm poor," whatever the excuse is, it's the excuse that holds you back!

We are all children of God, equal in His eyes, able to receive His love and let His light shine through us. Race, gender, stereotypes and economic limitations vanish in the face of this great truth.

Recipe for Achievement

Start with a large bowl of God's *Unconditional Love.* (Here's a special life-kitchen secret: this ingredient is present in every single dish you undertake. Acknowledging and accepting this truth guarantees the success of any recipe!)

Stir in cups of *Self-Awareness* and healthy *Self-Esteem.*

To this add a heaping cup of *Acceptance.*

Depending upon the specific goal of the recipe, balance measures of *Faith, Courage, Vision, Imagination, Energy,* and *Fun.*

Cook's Note: Be sure to keep your kitchen free of *Excuses.* These corrosive agents are subtle saboteurs of any creative undertaking.

Powerful Recycling

As human beings on the same road, we share certain experiences.
One that pains all of us at some time or other during the course of
our lives is the loss of a loved one, be it family member or friend. It's
almost impossible to prepare for it emotionally, but it is a transition
that needs to be managed if life is to go on, as it must. This is a
recipe for one way of coping with grief.

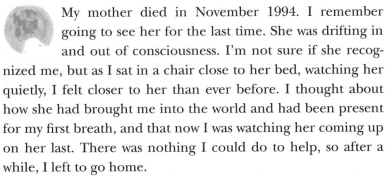 My mother died in November 1994. I remember going to see her for the last time. She was drifting in and out of consciousness. I'm not sure if she recognized me, but as I sat in a chair close to her bed, watching her quietly, I felt closer to her than ever before. I thought about how she had brought me into the world and had been present for my first breath, and that now I was watching her coming up on her last. There was nothing I could do to help, so after a while, I left to go home.

She died five days later. When I got the call, a tremendous sadness overwhelmed me, and I had no idea how I was going to process the grief. It felt more like the grief was going to have to process me, and I had no idea at the time what form that was going to take.

We had her cremated, and brought her ashes back home to Hawaii in a neatly tied box. Now, all her life my mother had been an incredible gardener. She loved to work in the garden, and she could grow anything! Once we got home, a plan began to take shape in my mind. It occurred to me that the thing to do was to find a nice plant—a special plant—for our garden, dig a place for it and mix some of my mother's ashes with the soil that would receive and nurture it. She could then continue as a part of something living! Just coming up with that idea somehow made the grief more manageable.

We put her box up on a shelf in my closet to wait for the time when we could all be together to carry out her memorial. Don't you know, one thing after another seemed to come along to get in the way—travel, business, busy-ness. Before we knew it, it was June 2000!

At that time, A&E *Biography* came out to Hawaii to do a piece on me, and my wonderful publicist, John Rosica came over to help coordinate events around the taping. He had known Ruby well and was also aware of what we had planned for her ashes. His first question was, "And how's Ruby doing?"

I had to answer, "John, she's just fine. She's in my closet upstairs on the shelf."

He said simply, "Well you know, it's time we planted her. What we're going to do is this: We're going to go to a nursery, and pick out a really special plant—today!"

I was delighted to be back on track with the plan because it was something I really had wanted to do.

We went to a charming neighborhood nursery and picked out a lovely little hibiscus plant—a kind of a hybrid they said would produce a most unusual flower: yellow on the outside and red on the inside. I thought that was pretty neat, because red had been Ruby's color—her birthstone was a ruby!

We brought the plant home. I brought Ruby down from my closet shelf upstairs and John and I dug the hole, removed the rocks, watered it, and got it ready for Ruby and her hibiscus. When it came time, I opened the box and looked at what remained of my mother. I took my hand, pushed it deep into the contents and then let her ashes sift through my fingers. It was a powerful moment, because while that was all that was left of my mother, she really wasn't there at all. Life had moved on.

We planted that baby hibiscus bush—named Ruby, of course. Today that bush has the most beautiful yellow and red blossems! I know Ruby is pleased. I think of her every time I see it. It's as if she's there to greet me everytime I come home. In her own way, she's still a part of our family!

Cook's Note: Recycling plays a vital part in any kitchen. Remember: Matter can neither be created nor destroyed—it simply evolves from one form to the next, and every transformation is meaningful in its own way. What is important is to find that meaning, incorporate it into your life, and then go forward from there.

The Ultimate Cook at Work

Barbara King is the minister and founder of Hillside Chapel in Atlanta, Georgia. She is a very powerful lady—about 6'7"—powerful in every respect. She is also a sensitive, beautiful soul. We became friends long ago when I had the occasion to speak at her church. I have since been a frequent guest speaker and we have stayed in close touch over the years.

Not long ago, my wonderful minister friend Barbara King came over to visit me here in Hawaii. One evening, after a fun-filled pizza dinner, we decided to make cookies. I always talk to the cookies when I slide them into the oven, and greet them with tunes on my kazoo when they emerge all hot and fragrant at the end of the process—I think that's important.

This particular evening, just as the first batch of cookies was ready to go in the oven, it occurred to me that Barbara is a mighty powerful pray-er. She can pray for days! Well you know, I had never had anybody pray over a batch of chocolate chip cookies before they were baked. So I called her over and told her what I wanted her to do. She obliged with a quick little simple prayer, something on the order of "Amen, God, thank you for these cookies."

I said "No, no, no, Barbara! You've got to give me more than that! I mean, I want you to offer a *prayer* for these cookies!"

So then she got down to business and *really* prayed over those cookies. She talked about cookies being sustenance, about cookies going out into the world to please and satisfy people.

She blessed the oven. She blessed the house. She thanked God, the Ultimate Creator . . . I mean, it was a powerful prayer! And you know, I swear those cookies really *did* taste special!

You may smile at this—it certainly makes me smile to remember it—but on a serious note, when those cookies came out of the oven after her prayer and I tasted the difference, that moment brought me right back to the fact that everything I do, everything I have and am, comes directly from God. I accept that great Truth joyfully and offer it to you. It is a tremendous source of strength, comfort, and encouragement.

How to Make Any Recipe "Special"

Mix together the ingredients a specific situation calls for.

Add *Acceptance* of your role as agent for God's creative process.

Blend in generous amounts of *Faith* and *Trust* in the fact that with God working through you, there's just no way your recipe can fail.

Proceed with *Confidence.*

Use *Generosity* in sharing the outcome of your success.

Vintage Wisdom

Children and the elderly have a lot in common. They waste no effort on trying to impress, and they are exceptionally honest. The big difference is that the wisdom of children comes out of their innocence, and the wisdom of the elderly, from years of experience.

The following story demonstrates the contents of a Personal Pantry successfully stocked over many years.

On October 20, 1999, in my hometown of Tallahassee, Florida, I had the privilege of joining Ms. Virgia McCray to celebrate her one hundred and first birthday, which was her last. Ms. Virgia signed my birth certificate over sixty-five years ago, and lived in the same house—built by her father—since she was eight years old.

She lived alone, but friends brought her food each day, cleaned her house, and made sure she was okay. She was sharp as a tack and enjoyed lively conversation. Her only concession to age was the walker she used as a result of severe arthritis in both legs. "Ain't nothin' wrong with my mind, it's my legs that don't work." She reads her mail, the newspaper and the Bible every day.

I was eager to learn from this centenarian, and throughout the day and evening that I spent with her on her birthday, I noted the following words of wisdom, and have matched them up with ingredients for a well-equipped Personal Pantry:

"Anything I ain't seen, I don' want to see. Anywhere I ain't been, I don't want to go." *Ability to Enjoy the Moment*

"I can't do what I used to do but I'm doing the best I can." *Self-Respect, Acceptance.* (Talk about growing old gracefully! How many of us know someone who wastes energy raging over the limitations age brings, instead of appreciating the things they can still manage?)

"Take care of your own business." *Good Judgment, Respect for Others, Responsibility.*

"Don't argue. Talk it over, then forget about it." *Communication, Positive Loving Attitude, Clarity.*

"If you don't give up, you won't give out." *Courage, Stick-to-it-iveness, Confidence.*

"Love everybody! Be good to everybody! Trust in God and everything will be alright!" *Faith, Trust, Unconditional Love, Positive Loving Attitude.*

 Cook's Note: We would all do well to stock our Personal Pantries as Ms. Virgia McCray did!

Stop and Smell the Cookies

Whenever anyone asks me what I like best about life, I tell them, "Breathing." Now, that sounds pretty basic, but the fact is, we tend to take breathing for granted. Let's face it: We can't do without it, but how often do we stop to appreciate it?

Here's a proven scientific fact: When we get stressed or frightened, one of the first things that gets compromised is our breathing. It's true: just when we most need big calming lungfuls of air, we shift into shallow panic breathing. With the brain shortchanged of oxygen, we are less able to think clearly, and become even more stressed and less rational. This tailspin does nothing to solve the problem at hand, and only serves to make things worse.

Observe yourself the next time you are in stressful circumstances: What happens to your breathing? Make a conscious choice to take three deep breaths, and see how that affects your ability to handle the situation. I can guarantee you'll be pleasantly surprised at the difference it makes.

You don't even have to be stressed to enjoy the simple pleasure of breathing! One of the best ways I know to really savor a big deep breath is to stand in the kitchen when a batch of cookies is in the oven. Or, even better, hold a cookie tray full of fresh-baked chocolate chip cookies and inhale. Breathe in . . . hold it . . . ahhhhhh!

Cook's Note: Your time in this kitchen called Life isn't all that long. Make the very most of it: Take the time to smell the cookies!!

Epilogue

As we come to the close of this special cookbook, let's take a break from baking and move into a different food group. Just to balance your diet, I'd like to offer you a little fruit.

 After my book, *Watermelon Magic: Seeds of Wisdom, Slices of Life* came out, I developed a set of short guidelines for life, using the letters of the word "watermelon." People have responded so enthusiastically that I want to share it with you here. After all, watermelon is a most nutritious food, and goes very well with a cookie or two.

Recipe for Watermelon Wisdom

(You'll recognize a number of our friendly Personal Pantry ingredients here!)

Whatever you believe creates your reality. (*Faith, Spirituality*)

Attitude is the magic word. (*Positive Loving Attitude*)

Together everyone achieves more—TEAM. (*Cooperation*)

Enthusiasm is the wellspring of life. (*Enthusiasm*)

Respect yourself and you will respect others. (*Respect*)

Make commitments, not excuses. (*Commitment*)

Every day can be a fun day. (*Fun!*)

Love is the answer, whatever the question. (*Unconditional Love*)

One day at a time. (*Vision, Focus, Tenacity, Problem Solving*)

Never give up or become a victim. (*Courage, Perseverance, Faith*)

Make sure your Personal Pantry is well stocked with the necessary ingredients. I'm sure there are all sorts of recipes just waiting for you to create terrific successes in your own life.

Above all, remember, regardless of the outcome of each individual recipe, it's all part of a larger Plan. With God as the Ultimate Cook, there is no such thing as a "mistake." Matter can never be created or destroyed, it is merely transformed from one state to another in the eternal forward motion of Life: The Cookie NEVER Crumbles!

Thanks for spending time in my kitchen.

ALOHA!

10

Time-Honored Cookie Recipes

Passing the Apron Over to You

Now it's time for you to go forth and make your own cookies! Just as with the other "recipes" in this book, use these recipes as blueprints, with the understanding that it's your privilege (responsibility, even!) as the Cook in your Kitchen to tweak and adjust the formulas to fit your own particular needs and tastes.

Enjoy!

Classic Chocolate Chip and Pecan Cookies

(a.k.a. The Cookie!)

Preheat oven to 375°F.

2 sticks (8 ounces) margarine	½ tsp. salt
2 eggs	¾ cup light brown sugar
1 tsp. *real* vanilla extract (Always use the real thing for genuine homemade taste!)	¾ cup granulated sugar
	2¼ cups all-purpose flour
	4 ounces pecan pieces
1 level tsp. baking soda	18 ounces semisweet chocolate chips (no shortcuts here, either!)

Thoroughly cream margarine, eggs, vanilla, brown and white sugars, baking soda, and salt. Add flour—*gently*! You don't want a snowstorm in your kitchen. Add pecans. Last, stir in the most important ingredient in chocolate chip cookies—the chocolate chips! Stir only until the chips are well integrated into the mix. Drop by teaspoonfuls onto a greased cookie sheet, about an inch apart. Baking time varies between 8 and 12 minutes, depending on your oven. I don't know about you, but when I bake cookies at home, I don't trust kitchen timers—I watch over them to see when they're done to perfection!

Makes 100 bite-sized cookies, if dropped by teaspoonfuls. Fewer if larger.

"Resourcefulness" Spice Cookies

Start with this recipe as written, but don't hesitate to play around with the balance of spices, depending on your preference. If you're short of ginger, then increase the cinnamon, or nutmeg—*Be resourceful!*

¾ cup shortening	½ tsp. ginger
1 cup sugar	1 tsp. cinnamon
¼ cup molasses	½ tsp. salt
1 egg	2 cups all-purpose flour
2 tsp. baking soda	granulated sugar
½ tsp. cloves	

Cream together the shortening, sugar and molasses until smooth. Add the egg; beat well.

Blend in the soda, cloves, ginger, cinnamon, salt, and flour; mix well. This makes a very stiff dough.

Chill the dough for about 1 hour (or longer). Form into 1-inch balls by rolling in the palm of your hand. Then roll the balls in granulated sugar and place on a cookie sheet about 2 inches apart. As the balls melt into perfect rounds, they will puff up and develop cracks.

Bake in a moderately hot oven, 375°F, for 10–12 minutes. The cookies will be soft while hot and will harden after cooling, so don't overcook!

Makes about 3 dozen.

"Stick-to-it-iveness" Peanut Butter Cookies

Just for fun, as you're making these, take a bite of peanut butter and pay attention to what it does to the roof of your mouth—talk about a graphic example of stick-to-it-iveness!

1 package yellow cake mix	**½ cup melted butter**
1 cup of crunchy peanut butter	**2 tbs. water**
	2 eggs, slightly beaten

Preheat oven to 350°F.

Combine all ingredients and mix well.

Drop by teaspoonfuls on ungreased cookie sheet. Press each cookie crisscross with a fork dipped in cold water.

Bake for 10–12 minutes.

Makes 48 small cookies.

"Creativity" Nut Balls

2 cups all-purpose flour
1 cup finely chopped nuts
(What kind of nuts? Try
pecan bits, walnut bits,
chopped almonds,
chopped peanuts, or see
what happens with
various combinations: *Be
creative!*)

¼ cup powdered sugar
¼ tsp. salt
½ tsp. vanilla
2 sticks (8 ounces) butter

Preheat oven to 350°F.
  Form into balls or crescents.
  (Or rectangles . . . or pyramids . . . BE CREATIVE!)
  Bake for 20 minutes or less. Do not let them brown.
  Roll in powdered sugar while still warm.
  Makes 24 cookies.

"Courage" Coconut Cookies

These offer a taste of Alohaland. They remind me of the courage it took to follow my dream and move to Hawaii. What dreams might they encourage you to follow?

2 sticks (8 ounces) butter	**1 cup shredded coconut**
¾ cup powdered sugar	**1 tsp. vanilla**
1½ cups all-purpose flour	**¼ tsp. almond extract**

Preheat oven to 350°F.

Mix butter and sugar.

Add flour, almond extract, coconut, and vanilla.

Shape into balls and flatten with a floured fork.

Place on a greased cookie sheet and bake for 15 minutes, or until edges are brown.

(*Optional:* for an even richer taste of Hawaii, you can add ¼–½ cup crushed macadamia nuts.)

Makes 48 cookies.

These cookies must always be served up with generous Aloha!